Quevedo: Los sueños

Critical Guides to Spanish Texts

EDITED BY J.E. VAREY AND A.D. DEYERMOND

QUEVEDO

Los sueños

R.M. Price

Senior Lecturer in Spanish
The University of Manchester

Grant & Cutler Ltd *in association with*
Tamesis Books Ltd 1983

4/1984
Span Cont

I.S.B.N. 84-499-6736-8
DEPÓSITO LEGAL: V. 2.749-1983

Printed in Spain by
Artes Gráficas Soler, S.A., Valencia
for
GRANT & CUTLER LTD
11 BUCKINGHAM STREET, LONDON, W.C.2

Contents

Preface

A brief summary of the complex editorial history of the *Sueños* of Quevedo will be found in the appendix, pp.80-83. The basic text is that of Barcelona, 1627; the Madrid 1631 edition, entitled *Juguetes de la niñez*, revises and corrects the earlier edition. For this Critical Guide I refer to the Maldonado edition of 1972 (*6*) which is based on Barcelona, 1627, and to the Clásicos Castellanos (*7*) when significant. Parenthetical page references are to *6*. Individual *Sueños* are referred to by shortened Barcelona 1627 titles (e.g. *Juicio*, *Alguacil*, *Infierno*, *Dentro*, and *Muerte*).

The figures in parenthesis in italic type refer to the numbered items in the Bibliographical Note; where necessary these are followed by page numbers, thus (*7*, pp.101-02).

I am grateful to the editors of the Critical Guides for their criticisms, help, and patience; errors of fact or judgement here are not attributable to them. The book is dedicated to Norma Price.

1. Introduction

The title of the first edition of the *Sueños* (*Sueños y discursos de verdades descubridoras de abusos, vicios y engaños en todos los oficios y estados del mundo*) indicates that the work which follows is an attack on aspects of society of the time, in the form of fictional dreams and visions; it is in fact a satire, as the general prologue confirms. It is necessary therefore to begin with some indications of the nature of satire. Satire is an attack in artistic form on persons, customs, institutions, or anything else to which the artist objects. It requires some artistic device or fictional framework for its expression (otherwise it would be simply denunciation), and satirists have used the comments or questions of ignorant strangers, visits to imaginary countries, or dreams or visions of visits to Hell or the kingdom of death, to carry out their satirical purposes. Satire ranges from personal insult, almost invective, to moral protest about the great follies or sins of men. At this level it is close to sermon, and some devotional writing attacks sin in a clearly satirical style before moving to positive moral recommendations (which are usually absent in satire). The satirist, an important and sometimes ambiguous figure, usually claims to see 'the world as it really is', even though he may in fact be expressing his own personal, social, and historical prejudices. He usually claims to be telling the truth, but we need not expect him to be fair or just; he claims to be driven irresistibly into satire and he often announces that his aim is moral, and certainly not directed at personal enemies. He usually attacks local targets, of his time and place; there is also a range of traditional targets: women, doctors, lawyers, the police, the army, tradesmen and shopkeepers, financiers (especially foreign), heretics, fake wise men, hypocrites, conservatives, revolutionaries, and (a favourite topic) other writers. The faults of these classes of person are obvious, and the satirist and his audience usually agree about them. Satirists compare the deplorable present sometimes with the nobler and purer past, and sometimes with the optimistically-viewed future. They often allude to their plain and straightforward style, and are, equally often, considerable artists, who use caricature, deflation and exaggeration techniques, burlesque description, invective, word-play, anecdotes, jokes, wit and irony. The satirist is often an ousider, but he sometimes realizes with sorrow that he is a sinner and a fool himself. Since satire has rarely made much difference to political, social, or moral conditions, it is often acknowledged to be ineffectual; it must therefore be written largely to amuse the reader, to demonstrate brilliance of style, and to gain a reputation for the author. Most of these characteristics can be identified in Quevedo's *Sueños*.[1]

As a seventeenth-century writer, Quevedo was educated in the Latin and to some extent the Greek classics. In his satirical poetry and prose he acknowledges the influence of Juvenal, Persius, Horace, and Martial. Margherita Morreale (*32*) has pointed out the influence of Lucian of Samosata in the *Sueños*. There was a strong medieval tradition of satire in Spain and Portugal (*5*), and Quevedo takes up a number of its themes (notably women, doctors, lawyers, and literary topics) in his own writing. In the sixteenth century some forceful satire in prose was written by Spaniards influenced by the writings of Erasmus, notably Alfonso de Valdés. A reading of Valdés's *Diálogo de Mercurio y Carón* (1528-29) shows that Quevedo's satire was not as forthright in some respects as that of Valdés (Quevedo never directly attacks the monarchy or the church, for instance), but his style is more demanding and brilliant and he rarely offers positive and constructive passages which might diminish the force of the attack.

Cervantes, who was an older contemporary of Quevedo and knew his work, refers to him as a withering satirist of contemporary poets. There is some common ground between the *Sueños* and some of the *Novelas ejemplares* (1613). In *El licenciado Vidriera* Cervantes, using a madman as his satirical device, touches briefly upon a number of topics (tradesmen,

[1] For a fuller account of satire see *4*; also A. Pollard, *Satire*, The Critical Idiom, 7 (London: Methuen, 1970).

poets, booksellers, apothecaries, tailors and doctors) also found in the *Sueños*. In the *Coloquio de los perros* Cervantes uses the device of two dogs who are mysteriously granted the gift of speech. One dog, telling his life story, surveys various low sectors of society in a disabused and satirical way. The *Coloquio de los perros* is however a more subtle work of art than any of the *Sueños* or any of Quevedo's satirical writing before the vast *Hora de todos*. Quevedo was a great satirical and moral poet, and most of the topics and some of the profound moral pronouncements of the *Sueños* are re-worked in his poetry, sometimes with close repetition of phrase. Before the *Sueños* he also wrote some short satirical prose pieces in the form of mock-decrees and instructions which anticipate a number of the satirical jokes against women, tradesmen, and annoying habits to be found in the *Sueños*. The second half of Quevedo's *Vida del buscón* (1626) is largely a satirical survey of some sectors of Madrid society. It seems likely that this was written at about the same time as the earlier *Sueños*, and some of the satirical material, the dense verbal style, and the general destruction of false appearances occur in both.

One other area of Quevedo's prose writing is relevant to a study of the *Sueños*. In the period before the first edition of the *Sueños* he wrote some distinguished devotional prose. *La cuna y la sepultura* (1612, 1630) begins with a denunciation of the vanities and misapprehensions of sinful man, in a notably vigorous and satirical style. The later chapters are more positive and doctrinal in tone. Evidently the moral style of some passages of the *Sueños* is not merely a matter of variety. The *Política de Dios, gobierno de Cristo* (Part I, 1626) is a series of lessons for kings, based upon Quevedo's interpretations of incidents in the life of Christ. It is a 'mirror for princes' with strong theological overtones, but contemporary readers, who made it into a best-seller, may well have seen it as a satirical work. The author was, after all, an eye-witness of the royal court in the reign of Felipe III and his corrupt minister, Lerma. At the very least it implies that the previous, and perhaps the present, king was less than perfect as a ruler. The *Sueños* seem to be lacking in specific political satire; some of Quevedo's political criticisms may have been expressed in this more devotional and respectable form.

2. The Sueños

a) *Sueño del juicio final (Sueño de las calaveras)*

This is the first and earliest of the *Sueños*, written apparently in 1605. The version published in 1627 was subjected to some changes when it was republished in 1631 (see Appendix). Quevedo dedicates the work to the distinguished statesman and nobleman, the Conde de Lemos (to whom Cervantes was to dedicate the second part of *Don Quixote*). It was usual at that time to dedicate works to a dignitary, because his name was thought to give authority and respectability to a book, and because the dedication might attract (or be a response to) his patronage. Dedications also gave the author the opportunity to indicate the nature and the intention of the book. Such indications were sometimes put into a note to the reader, and were, as we shall see, sometimes clearly tongue-in-cheek. Quevedo refers conventionally here to the 'desnudas verdades' of his work, a claim often and quite inaccurately made for satire.

Quevedo begins by quoting classical authorities for the divine origin and significance of dreams. There was an important tradition of dream literature in the medieval period, and dream-poetry was important in the classical and Biblical traditions (see *40*, which is further discussed below). In this tradition the writer sometimes tells how he fell asleep over a book which to some extent triggered off or influenced the dream. Here Quevedo says he fell asleep over a book about the end of the world and the Second Coming of Christ, and so he dreamed about the Last Judgement. He attenuates the seriousness of this by wordplay about *juicio* ('judgement', 'commonsense') and the insane reputation of poets, and then adds another traditional view of dreams: that they are about the dreamer's waking preoccupations. This is, therefore, a somewhat confusing beginning in which Quevedo establishes the literary and fictional nature of his 'desnudas verdades' and also makes a claim for their seriousness.

Quevedo[2] sees an angel blowing a trumpet for the Day of Judgement; souls and bodies come together to prepare for judgement and it becomes apparent that the work is satirical, although not wholly so. He reacts with amusement to the sinners he sees, and invites the reader to react in the same way. Some sinners, however, here and in later *Sueños*, are seen with great seriousness. Various sinners flee from the parts of their bodies by which they sinned on earth, and this leads to satirical jabs: 'los lujuriosos no querían que los hallasen sus ojos por no llevar al tribunal testigos contra sí, y los ladrones y matadores gastaban los pies en huir de sus mismas manos' (73). The mildly witty connection between 'pies' and 'manos' is a foretaste of the punning style of the *Sueños*. Quevedo goes through a number of his satirical targets: notaries, misers, merchants, women, constables, a judge, innkeepers, tailors, a bookseller, until he begins to describe the judgement scene before the throne of God. This is of course described in reverent terms, but he quickly returns to satire, on doctors, who are accused by the natural ills of having killed more people than disease itself. The sudden changes of tone between grave and flippant are characteristic of the *Sueños*, although they are at their most disconcerting here. Quevedo briefly considers historical and Biblical figures, such as Adam, the Apostles, Herod and Pilate, but soon turns to a more prosaic target, a hapless fencing theorist and teacher, based upon a personal enemy of Quevedo. He, along with a number of other figures in the *Sueños*, is also satirized in the *Buscón*. The devils themselves laugh at his pretensions; part of the joke, and this is a humorous idea often used in the *Sueños*, is that the fencing teacher is still absorbed with his skills even after death. Judas Iscariot, to play a bigger

---

[2] A distinction must be made here. When Quevedo addresses the Conde de Lemos he is the real Francisco de Quevedo (1580-1645); when he defends the significance of dreams, or addresses the reader, he is Quevedo the author or writer; as he moves through his own narrations he is Quevedo the narrator. The person and the writer tend to blur into one another; the writer and the narrator also tend to overlap. I discuss this problem later (pp.53-54).

part in a later *Sueño*, is quickly condemned, and Quevedo turns to a piemaker, accused here and later of putting all the animals of Noah's ark, as well as human flesh, into his pies. After some satirical fun at Virgil (seen in the medieval tradition as a wizard, not as the great poet) and Orpheus, we have a characteristic passage attacking a miser. This sinner has the Ten Commandments read to him, and sardonically — his ruling passion undiminished by the occasion — declares that he has respected them: 'Leyó el primero: "Amar a Dios sobre todas las cosas", y dijo que él solo aguardaba a tenerlas todas para amar a Dios sobre ellas' (81). His defence is based on cynicism and wordplay.

The peculiar jumble of social sinners and major historical figures appropriate to the dream of a seventeenth-century satirist continues, with the use of wordplay. A 'farandulero' claims that he is a 'cómico' (an actor of higher rank) and is denounced by a devil, who reveals the truth of his status; similarly, 'escribanos' try to claim the title of 'secretarios' (82). Occasionally, there is a more serious note: Christians are more severely dealt with than pagans, and some notaries point out that it is not their fault if they were baptized but that of their parents. Quevedo evidently expected his reader to see a satirical point without much explanation; he could draw upon a mass of commonly understood assumptions (all lawyers are venal, all tradesmen are cheats, all doctors are incompetent). In this convention, all tavern-keepers water their wine, and whatever the seriousness of this crime, here they are damned for it: '[muchos taberneros] fueron acusados de que habían muerto mucha cantidad de sed a traición, vendiendo agua por vino. Estos venían confiados en que habían dado a un hospital siempre vino puro para las misas' (83). Behind the mock-gravity of the accusation ('muerto … a traición') about a minor fraud, there is a deeper note: good actions do not cancel out bad ones; we shall meet people who are too confident of God's mercy in a later *Sueño*.

Quevedo gives us a glimpse of hardened sinners in this still comic hell: some unchaste women who have been devoted to the name of the Virgin Mary, but not to her example, are judged (the reader may remember the mock-piety of the harlots in Cervantes's *Rinconete y Cortadillo*); one admits guilt, and says 'Ojalá supiera que me había de condenar, que no hubiera oído misa los días de fiesta' (85). This repentance for what were good acts in life is part of the paradoxical attitude of the life of hell; it will be exploited in later *Sueños*. We next meet Judas Iscariot, Mohammed, and Martin Luther; the last two both claim to be Judas, since only he stands any chance on the Day of Judgement, as Judas makes clear in his defence: 'Señor, yo soy Judas; y bien conocéis vos que soy mucho mejor que éstos: porque si os vendí, remedié al mundo; y éstos vendiéndose a sí y a otros, lo han destruido todo' (85). Quevedo's satirical structures sometimes allow maligned figures to defend themselves, as Iventosch (*25*) observes. In *Infierno* Judas is to defend himself with considerable force.

We have another glimpse of an astronomer, another figure who appears in later *Sueños*, and the tribunal comes to an end. Quevedo sees a few more petty sinners, a lawyer, a doctor and an apothecary, at whom he laughs, and his laughter wakes him, even though, as he points out, the dream is a sad one. We return to the outer framework of this first *Sueño* with remarks from the writer to the patron, and, of course, to the reader: 'Sueños son éstos, que si se duerme vuestra excelencia sobre ellos, verá que, por ver las cosas como las veo, las esperará como las digo' (186).

Juicio contains in potential a great deal of what is to come in other *Sueños*. Clearly there is in this first one some haste, some dashing from joke to joke, some disconcerting unevenness of tone. Quevedo is to work over a large proportion of the ideas here in later *Sueños*, most notably in *Infierno*; he will develop them more powerfully and wittily, and considerably heighten a moral and sermon-like manner barely hinted at here. We should observe here the literary device (a dream, an eye-witness account) which makes the satire possible; the social and ethical lines of attack and defence; the chaotic organization, appropriate to a dream; the personal reactions, not yet inter-ventions, of the narrator; and the need to read each sentence with care, for its ironies, its rapid allusions and wordplay.

b) *El alguacil endemoniado* (*El alguacil alguacilado*)

The second of the *Sueños* is dated 1607 by Astrana Marín (*10*) and 1605-08 by Maldonado (*6*); it was therefore written around the date of the first part of *Don Quixote* and of some of the *Novelas ejemplares* of Cervantes. It is respectfully dedicated, again, to the Conde de Lemos. We should note in Quevedo's address to him the linking of the writer and devils, since Quevedo is to refer to it later: 'Bien sé que a los ojos de vuestra excelencia es más endemoniado el autor que el sujeto' (87). Quevedo goes on to prepare the discourse with a mock-parallel between kinds of devils, as distinguished in a book by Michael Psellus,[3] and kinds of constable, whose notorious cowardice and corruption is often attacked in the *Sueños*. Psellus related devils to elements and locations, and Quevedo does this for constables:

> los subterráneos, que están debajo de la tierra, son los escudriñadores de vidas, y fiscales de honras, y levantadores de falsos testimonios, de bajo de tierra sacan qué acusar, y andan siempre desenterrando los muertos y enterrando los vivos. (88)

'Desenterrar los muertos' also meant to slander the dead; 'enterrar los vivos' meant to imprison or execute the living. Quevedo, as we see in the *Sueños*, brings back some at least of the dead, and allows them to defend themselves and to attack and demolish the living.

After the modest dedication and the mock-erudition, Quevedo turns to the 'pious reader', although the suggestion of ingratiation is at once deflated by wordplay. He discusses writers and non-writers and their reasons. Some do not write because they fear evil tongues. Quevedo excepts himself from this category; wise men will not speak evil of him, nor will ignorant men, lest they reveal their own evil or ignorance. His attitude is defiant, but he clearly has an eye on the reader. He ends his note cautiously and conventionally — he is attacking only evil

---

[3] Michael Psellus (1018-78?) the Byzantine scholar and Platonist wrote a book about devils translated into Latin by Marsilio Ficino (see *7*, vol.I, p.57n).

ministers of justice, subject to the correction of the authorities;
satirists were not unwilling to draw attention to the difficulties
of the genre.

After this emphasis on writers and readers, Quevedo begins
his narration. He says that he went into a church to see a clergyman, the *licenciado* Calabrés, his confessor (a fictitious figure,
based apparently upon a real person of different name, who was
finally expelled from Spain by the Holy Office). Quevedo
presents him by a *tour de force* description which has been
admired by critics, and concludes by describing him plainly as a
hypocrite. He is a 'lanzador de diablos' and is trying to cast a
devil out of a man. The 'evil spirit' denies that he is in a man; it
is an *alguacil,* whom, since he shares the general disdain for
them, he wishes to leave. He admits that devils and constables
have features in common, but with comical snobbery insists that
constables are worse. The relationship is complex: it is hell for a
devil to find himself in a constable; he can, however, talk only
with the tongue of a constable. Calabrés tries to silence him. So
far, we have a fictitious narrative, a fictitious priest, who is a
hypocrite, in a church (where the truth is told), a devil-possessed
alguacil (devils tell lies and so do *alguaciles*); we do not know
whether a devil is speaking through the *alguacil,* or whether a
madman and a constable is speaking. Satire is often placed in the
mouth of a madman, as we see in Cervantes's *El licenciado
Vidriera* and in *Don Quixote.* Calabrés decides to silence the
devil because he is slandering law officers, who keep order and
help people to be good. Given that there is often a link between
crime and sin, this is an acceptable reason, but Calabrés is a
hypocrite. Quevedo, as the narrator, wants to know what he has
to say. He is a friend of the priest and confesses to him, although
he knows him to be unworthy. We also remember that the real
Quevedo is regarded as bedevilled by his patron; he has links in
fact both with Calabrés and with the demon-constable. Quevedo
twice says that he wonders at the *sutilezas* of the devil (not the
truths or the perceptions, we note) and he asks Calabrés to allow
the devil to speak. We thus have one speaker (devil or constable)
and two hearers, one indignant and the other amused and
curious. The devil reports on hell: there are poets there (like

Quevedo, who is more involved now than he was on the Day of Judgement) and there is some playful satire on them; they are pagan, they are punished by hearing other poets praised; their artistic worries continue as part of their punishment. The devil declares that sinners are to some extent grouped together by means of wit:

> Un ciego, que quiso encajarse con los poetas [blind men used to sing doggerel in the street] fue llevado a los enamorados, por serlo todos. Otro, que dijo 'yo enterraba difuntos', fue acomodado con los pasteleros ... Uno vino por unas muertes, y está con los médicos ... los necios están con los verdugos. Y un aguador, que dijo había vendido agua fría, fue llevado con los taberneros. (94)

A more conventional organization of hell would no doubt have placed similar sinners together, as they are in *Infierno*; clearly, Quevedo's view of hell is a trifle flippant. These odd juxtapositions are based on satirical considerations obvious to the contemporary reader; the serious elements of the Day of Judgement, and of the later *Infierno*, are absent; this hell does not inspire horror.

Quevedo listens with interest, and asks about lovers (he is one) in hell. The devil takes a comic and disabused view of lovers: they love themselves, their own words, their deeds; some even love women, although these are few, women being, satirically speaking, what they are. Distantly, the reader perceives that love and self-love, selfishness, and pride are all connected. Quevedo's irritation at the scandal and the futility of 'amantes de monjas' is also expressed in the *Buscón*. The devil expresses some of his own prejudices, since devils have their standards; they loathe lovers of old women, and are annoyed at Hieronymus Bosch, whose paintings Quevedo had evidently seen (*26*). The devil comments on the common use of phrases like '¡Pues el diablo te lleve!'; Quevedo is to consider common speech in more depth in the last of the *Sueños*. There follows a rare note of political satire. Quevedo asks if there are kings in hell, and the devil says there are; kings are particularly exposed to extremes of vice. He uses metaphor and wordplay here:

> Uno se condena por la crueldad, y, matando y desterrando
> los suyos, es una ponzoña ... y una peste real de sus reinos;
> otros se pierden por la codicia, haciendo amazonas sus
> villas y ciudades a fuerza de grandes pechos ... y otros se
> van al infierno por terceras, y se condenan por poderes,
> fiándose de infames ministros. (97)

Quevedo is not too specific (this work is dedicated to one of
the king's ministers) but he was writing in the time of the Duque
de Lerma, and the *Sueños* were published in the time of the
Conde-Duque de Olivares.[4] We note here the idea, often found
in the *Sueños*, of groups of sinners — kings bring others with
them. In the 1627 version the devil excludes Spain from
reference, although he mentions sumptuous building, a
weakness of Lerma; in 1631 the passage was corrected, and is
more sympathetic to kings and favourites (7, vol.I, p.76).

The devil turns to merchants in hell, and the accusation that
the Genoese are exploiting Spain's American gold; and to
judges, and we again see the idea of dependent and subaltern
sinners encouraging each other in the range of law officers who
accompany them to hell (99). Quevedo, or Calabrés, who is also
taking part in the conversation, protests, and the devil tells a
traditional satirical tale about Truth and Justice on earth, one
struck dumb, and other other retired to heaven. This seems to
mark the beginning of the overtly preaching manner in the
Sueños. The devil applies his story to the constables' staffs of
the world, and ends his remarks with an attack upon the police.
All men steal, with different parts of their bodies, or by different
means; only the constable is a complete stealing-machine. The
rapid descent from a story of moral nature to satire against a
disdained and hated figure is characteristic of the style of the
Sueños. Quevedo makes no comment here on the paradox of a
devil preaching; he is to explain this at the end of this *Sueño* and

---

[4] Lerma, the favourite and minister of Felipe III, was notoriously corrupt;
Olivares, the minister of Felipe IV, was honest, but his power was resented by the
nobility (2; 3). Favourites were often attacked by satirists who did not wish to
attack the king directly.

to use it powerfully in the next. Even here there is some
ambiguity in the devil's remarks; he would want us to despair of
justice and truth, and not all his alleged thieves are necessarily
pernicious.

Quevedo enquires about women in hell and hears that they are
now inhabitants rather than the punished. Some cynical and
traditional points are made, dating from *The Greek Anthology*
and Martial, especially about vain and heavily made-up old
women. There is a short positive passage. The devil is to some
extent guided by Quevedo's enquiries, and when he asks about
the poor, the devil has never heard of them; the things of the
world condemn men, and these have nothing. The devil notes
that men can be devils to each other in life by means of flattery,
treachery, and envy. He ends his remarks in the manner of a
sermon, appropriate to the church in which all this has taken
place:

> ¿Cuál de vosotros sabe estimar el tiempo y poner precio al
> día, sabiendo que todo lo que pasó lo tiene la muerte en su
> poder, y gobierna lo presente y aguarda lo porvenir, como
> todos ellos? (102)

Quevedo returns to what might be called the inner framework,
Calabrés versus the devil-possessed constable: 'Cuando el diablo
predica, el mundo se acaba. ¿Pues cómo, siendo tú padre de la
mentira — dijo Calabrés — dices cosas que bastan a convertir
una piedra?' (102). He sees the paradox in a devil, who is a liar,
preaching to Quevedo, himself, and the reader, who have indeed
heard things which should convert them. The devil declares that
he has told the truth in order to do harm. Good things can be
used for evil purposes, and here he is candid about them; his
hearers cannot now say that they were not told. He comments on
their reaction — tears of grief rather than repentance, tiredness
of sin rather than loathing of it. Satirists are usually aware of
their ultimate failure to convert hearers and readers. Calabrés
denies this accusation, and, against Quevedo's wish, persists in
trying to silence him. There is some ambiguity here, akin to the
kind of ambiguity we often find in Cervantes. Calabrés is doing

good by silencing a devil, since he is in possession of an *alguacil*, who, according to Calabrés, a clergyman, has a soul to lose. But Calabrés is a hypocrite who might therefore be interested in the suppression of the truth, if the devil is telling the truth. It might be better for the devil to go on speaking, since news from hell might have a salutary effect; but the devil is sceptical about the effect of his own words, and satire and the reports and preaching of a devil are not necessarily the whole truth. Quevedo still has his outer framework to use. He addresses 'vuestra excelencia' (the Conde de Lemos, who thinks Quevedo is 'endemoniado') and invites him to consider the whole narration and not its narrator (whether Quevedo or the devil). No doubt we as readers should consider, as the last lines indicate, the testimony and not the testifier — the devil's report, even though devils are normally liars, and Quevedo's satire, even though he is a fiction writer.

The second *Sueño* is clearly an improvement on the first. The divine elements of the Last Judgement of the first *Sueño* were embarrassing, and were made absurd by the corrections of the *Juguetes*. Some people had to be saved and this diminished the satire. Here there is still some disorganized movement from topic to topic but there is also evidence of some grouping of the material: lovers, poets, women are together and are given a more thorough treatment. The main satirical device, a devil who reports to Quevedo and answers questions about hell, gives Quevedo control of the narrative. The ambiguity of the framework makes the reader think about the nature of evidence, the reliability of witnesses, about fiction and satire, and yet deduce a moral lesson. The wordplay is more controlled, Quevedo is learning to put a necessary positive note into his satire (the short discourse on the poor is an example); the moral note is to be developed powerfully in the next two *Sueños*.

c) *Sueño del infierno* (*Las zahurdas de Plutón*)

This is in many ways the most significant and successful of the *Sueños*. In the *Carta a un amigo suyo* Quevedo notes that this is the third of the *Sueños*, so it seems likely that the first three were written in this order. He refers to his own wit ('las pocas fuerzas de mi ingenio'), his hopes for either gratitude or praise for writing, and to unspecified literary enemies. In his *Prólogo al ingrato y desconocido lector* he parodies the conventional approach to the reader, calling him evil and perverse. He makes the usual satirist's claim to straightforwardness: 'ya desengañado, quiero hablar contigo claramente' (106). He is flippant about the reader's reaction — 'si te parece largo, en tu mano está: toma el infierno que te bastare y calla.' He then somewhat contradicts himself and refuses to promise either clarity or amusement: 'Si fuere oscuro, nunca el infierno fue claro; si triste y melancólico, yo no he prometido risa' (106). The note ends with conventional protestations that he is attacking vices in general, not persons, but also with some independence: 'y al fin, si te agradare el discurso tú te holgarás, y si no, poco importa, que a mí de ti ni de él se me da nada.' The mockery of literary conventions, the parody of the usual deferential and defensive attitudes to the reader, the off-hand indications of a possible moral lesson, the wordplay, the general air of tongue-in-cheek, all indicate a writer at a high point of confidence.

At the beginning of the discourse Quevedo changes rapidly from the writer, looking back again to the first two *Sueños* and reminding the reader of the unreal nature of dreams and the lying propensities of devils, to the narrator, who proceeds to tell us of his vision:

> Yo, que en el *Sueño del juicio* vi tantas cosas y en *El alguacil endemoniado*, oí parte de las que no había visto, como sé que los sueños, las más veces, son burla de la fantasía y ocio del alma, y que el diablo nunca dijo verdad, por no tener cierta noticia de las cosas que justamente nos esconde Dios, vi, guiado del Angel de mi Guarda, lo que se sigue, por particular providencia de Dios; que fue para traerme, en el miedo, la verdadera paz. (106)

He does not tell us any more about the 'verdadera paz' to which his vision brings him; there may be some echo here and in the first scene of the narrative of the words of St Augustine:

'inquietum est cor nostrum donec requiescat in te' (My heart is restless until it rests in Thee). Quevedo's narrative opens in a peaceful pastoral place (another conventional feature of medieval dream literature) in which he is uneasy; the pastoral life, and this world, are not enough. He sees two allegorical roads: one, a beggar explains, is the strait and narrow path of virtue, on which people travel with suffering in the course of their lives. The beggar, significantly, avoids useless convers- ations as a waste of time (talkers are part of the entourage of death in *Muerte*). Quevedo joins the other road, where he finds all the best people. He thus depicts himself as one of the weak and sinful; this is a conventional satirical device, to disarm the criticism that the satirist sees himself as superior to his fellow men. After this strong allegorical opening, some of the satire seems disconcertingly trivial; the tailors, the doctors, and the beards affected by lawyers serve to remind us of which road we are on; for doctors he uses military and lethal metaphor: 'no digo eso porque fuese menor el batallón de los doctores, a quien nueva elocuencia llama ponzoñas graduadas, pues se sabe que en sus universidades se estudia para tósigos' (109). The allegory becomes more complex; there is a connection between the paths, and people are easily inveigled from one to the other. Hypocrites are seen as travelling on a path apparently parallel to that of virtue, and Quevedo takes the opportunity to attack false holy men. He notes their ability to pervert good things for evil purposes: penitence, fasting, and mortifications are a 'noviciado del infierno' for them (109). They also contrive to misuse the truth: 'diciendo que son unos indignos y grandísimos pecadores y los más malos de la tierra, llamándose jumentos, engañan con la verdad, pues siendo hipócritas, lo son al fin' (110).

This reminds us of the hypocritical *licenciado* Calabrés and anticipates the attack on hypocrisy in the next *Sueño*; the true and the false are a great underlying theme of the *Sueños*.

False holy men have their devotees, usually female, so Quevedo is ready to attack women, a traditional target of the satirist. He also refers to true saints to whom women should direct their devotions, and so makes a positive point in the middle of his satire. The passage was considerably modified in the *Juguetes* version, and the reference to specific saints was omitted (7, vol.I, pp.101-02).

Quevedo continues with another example of positive and negative conduct. He satirizes the false, drunken and boastful soldiers he sees, and mentions in contrast real soldiers, who reproach and exhort their fellows with considerable eloquence, declaring that soldiers should fight for noble causes without hope of reward. In the 1627 version at least, satirical reality asserts itself; the bad soldiers are not moved, and they plunge into a tavern. Boastful soldiers are a traditional target of satire and the discipline and conduct of soldiers were a constant interest of seventeenth-century Spanish writers. Quevedo discusses military morale and discipline in his poetry and in the *Política de Dios*, II.

After some satire of minor targets, venal and luxury-loving women and miserable married men, Quevedo arrives in hell, followed by all that he had known on earth. At this second stage of the narration we see that he has been revealing the satirical truth on the roads of life; he will continue to be an observer and commentator in hell. No punishment is assigned to Quevedo, but he implies that some of the lessons learned apply to him.

The interlacing of serious and trivial satire, of sarcasm and moral pronouncement, continues. Tailors are a traditional target of satire, apparently because they stole the cloth brought to them by customers. Quevedo follows this tradition; we can only speculate that a minor and hard-up nobleman would resent tradesmen who represented the necessity for expensive false appearances, who might be cheating him, and to whom he might owe money. Tailors are here shovelled into hell, as fuel for the fires.

Quevedo next meets a bookseller burning in the flames of the place. This old acquaintance is in hell for the 'malas obras' of other people:

> Pues es tanta mi desgracia, que todos se condenan por las malas obras que han hecho, y yo y todos los libreros nos condenamos por las malas obras que hacen los otros y porque hicimos barato de los libros en romance y

traducidos de latín, sabiendo ya con ellos los tontos lo que
encarecían en otros tiempos los sabios; que ya hasta el
lacayo latiniza y hallarán a Horacio en castellano en la
caballeriza. (116)

He is then tormented by the smoke from his own books and
readings from them, and Quevedo wonders what punishment
may be reserved for authors (we are to meet some later). The
passage is characteristic of the *Sueños* in its apparent playfulness
and real seriousness. Books were thought to have an effect upon
moral life, both personally and nationally. Quevedo also had an
elitist, not to say snobbish, attitude to their diffusion, not
uncommon in his time. Works are translated and this is a
dilution and a danger to true learning; books may fall into the
wrong hands. False learning and pedantry are often targets of
satire, and we remember that Cervantes is also greatly interested
in books and their largely uncontrollable effects upon readers.
This incident reminds us of the importance of books and readers
in the *Sueños*, where many kinds of more obvious sinner or
criminal are not mentioned at all.

We return to the purely social level: Quevedo meets a group of
coachmen who are furious at being in hell. This is a
denunciation of the immoral opportunities offered by their
coaches, and so it is also an attack upon women, who were
enthusiastic passengers for their own purposes. In seventeenth-
century terms this would have been funny; the coachmen claim
to have supplied hell with many a *condenada* in mint condition,
and they expect preferential treatment, even reward, rather than
the beatings they appropriately receive (and professionally criti-
cize). The irony is sharp; hell is after all a place of reward for
their efforts.

Quevedo next visits a cold area of hell, and there finds
'bufones, truhanes, y juglares chocarreros' who are tormented
with stale jokes, *frialdades*. These are mainly flatterers, toadies,
and professional spongers, and we have a sudden glimpse of the
humiliations suffered by such people in life (119). Quevedo uses
the technique of mislocation here; that is, he puts apparently
different sinners together because he satirically perceives the

basic similarity of their sins (in *Alguacil* he did this on a purely
verbal basis). Corrupt judges and men thought to be honourable
but who were in fact flatterers are therefore found alongside
clowns and parasites. Quevedo's hell is a place where the truth
of matters is revealed. We also observe that the devils comment
to Quevedo on the world he comes from: 'bien mirado, en el
mundo todos sois bufones, pues los unos andáis riendo de los
otros, y en todos, como digo, es naturaleza, y en unos pocos,
oficio' (119). After a jab at cobblers, Quevedo repeats earlier
satirical accusations made at piemakers (see *Juicio*, pp.79, 80),
accusations which combine dietary taboos, public health,
resentment at tradesmen, and a desire to be witty and shocking.
When Quevedo turns to merchants it is apparent that he is not
interested in the defence offered by one of them (defensive
statements are allowed to more worthy figures, it seems). He
proceeds to a denunciation of these shopkeepers based upon
wordplay and irreverent allusion (122; the passage is considered
in detail below, p.67). Quevedo calls this speech 'propriedades';
the devils are telling the truth in hell. Their denunciation extends
into an attack upon the vanity of man, which drives him to buy
worthless things. Quevedo repeated this connection between
vanity, foolishness, and sin elsewhere, notably in his sonnet 'Si
el mundo amaneciera cuerdo un día' (*12*, p.573).

He moves on, attracted by the sound of laughter, unexpected
in hell, as he points out, but laughter is one of the aims of the
satirist, and it can be regarded as one of the punishments of hell.
We are to accept, once again, that some people arrive here
unpurged of their ruling passions, and unaware of their sins.
The devils are laughing at two *hidalgos* who have arrived; when
one boasts of his descent, a devil beats him, and begins a dis-
illusioning discourse, close to a sermon, on honour, nobility,
and valour. Quevedo is using commonplaces here from the satire
and the moral discourses of the time; the peculiar twist here is
the preacher and the place:

en la chancillería del infierno arrúgase el pergamino y
consúmense las letras, y, el que en el mundo es virtuoso,
ése es el hidalgo, y la virtud es la ejecutoria que acá

respetamos, pues aunque descienda de hombres viles y
bajos, como él con divinas costumbres se haga digno de
imitación, se hace noble a sí y hace linaje para otros.
Reímonos acá de ver los que ultrajáis a los villanos, moros
y judíos, como si en éstos no cupieran las virtudes que
vosotros despreciáis. (123)

It is odd to find a devil in hell admitting respect for virtue and
preaching about true nobility, but it is obviously the reader who
is to learn the lesson. The sermon proceeds in the accepted
rhetorical manner ('Pues, ¿qué diré de la honra mundana?...',
124), dividing the attack into three topics: nobility, honour, and
valour. The attack upon honour, as critics have noted (*8*, *34*), is
ambiguous. The devil denounces honour as a motivation of
conduct (the whole passage should be read):

Y llegado a ver lo que es la honra mundana, no es nada.
Por la honra no come el que tiene gana donde le sabría
bien. Por la honra se muere la viuda entre dos paredes. Por
la honra, sin saber qué es hombre, ni qué es gusto, se pasa
la doncella treinta años casada consigo misma. Por la
honra, la casada le quita a su deseo cuanto pide. Por la
honra pasan los hombres la mar. (124)

Evidently, some of the things listed here are laudable. The
devil may be deliberately confusing motivations, and he is not
necessarily an advocate for the truth, even though in hell devils
usually speak the satirical truth. Honour can be misused as a
motivation, as can most noble causes. If a woman refuses to
marry out of *honra*, it may be snobbery on her part, or it may be
virtue, which the devil would be against. This infernal preacher
concludes the first division of his discourse witheringly:

hase de advertir que las cosas de más valor en vosotros son
la honra, la vida, y la hacienda. La honra está junto al culo
de las mujeres; la vida en manos de los doctores, y la
hacienda, en pluma de los escribanos: ¡desvaneceos, pues,
bien mortales! (124)

Quevedo reacts on behalf of the reader, and makes his satirical device clear: 'Dije yo entre mí —¡Y cómo se echa de ver que esto es el infierno, donde, por atormentar a los hombres en amarguras, les dicen las verdades!' (125).

The devil makes a similar contemptuous attack upon bravery — it is based upon fear, greed, or passion. He ends the discourse with a satirical commonplace, repeated by Quevedo elsewhere (the source may be Erasmus; the idea is also used by Lope de Vega, Mateo Alemán, and Antonio de Guevara) which reminds us of the importance attached to language by all satirists; men misname things: 'así, los hombres, que todo lo entendéis al revés, bobo llamáis al que no es sedicioso, alborotador, maldiciente; y sabio llamáis al mal acondicionado, perturbador y escandaloso' (125).[5] We should note the phrase 'entendéis al revés'; to attain a correct opinion about the nature of things was an ambition of the Stoics who inspired Quevedo's writing in poetry and prose.

After this heightened passage some light relief is needed. There is an attack on *dueñas*, hated by most of the satirists of the time (although Cervantes, and Quevedo in *Muerte*, allow them some defence). *Dueñas* are the frogs of hell, and Quevedo reacts with laughter at this point. After this come two sombre passages; the chaotic geography of hell and the unguided visit allow these changes of tone. He sees fathers who increased their wealth and earned themselves damnation in order to leave their sons rich; when the devils jeer at them, they howl, and Quevedo, for the first time of his visit, reacts with pity: 'se pusieron todos a aullar y a darse de bofetones. Hiciéronme lástima, no lo pude sufrir, y pasé adelante' (127).

---

[5] J.E. Varey deals with this topic in Lope de Vega's *Fuenteovejuna*, and quotes examples from Guevara and Alemán, in *La inversión de valores en 'Fuenteovejuna'*, Lectiones, V (Santander: Universidad Internacional de Menéndez Pelayo, 1980). See also the interesting studies of Helen F. Grant, 'El mundo al revés', in *Hispanic Studies in Honour of Joseph Manson*, ed. D.M. Atkinson and A.H. Clarke (Oxford: Dolphin, 1972), pp.119-37; 'The World Upside-Down', in *Studies in Spanish Literature of the Golden Age Presented to Edward M. Wilson*, ed. R.O. Jones (London: Tamesis Books, 1973), pp.103-35; and 'Images et gravures du monde à l'envers dans leurs relations avec la pensée et la littérature espagnoles', in *L'Image du monde renversé et ses représentations littéraires et para-littéraires de la fin du XVIe siècle au milieu du XVIIe*, ed. M. Jean Lafond and Augustin Redondo (Paris: Vrin, 1979), pp.17-33.

In the next incident, Quevedo takes on the role of the uncomprehending questioner. He cannot understand why people have been damned for saying 'Dios es piadoso'; a devil explains that this undeniable statement is not a guarantee against the consequences of sin. Quevedo requires clarification here (this is to be the main device of the next *Sueño*); the devil preaches directly: 'No merece la piedad de Dios quien, sabiendo que es tanta, la convierte en licencia y no en provecho espiritual' (125). Quevedo again reacts for the reader: '¿Esto se ve y se oye en el infierno? ¡Ah, lo que aprovechará allá uno de estos escarmentados!' (128).

After some fun at the expense of 'los putos, las viejas y los cornudos' we return to the didactic and moral note. Some of the damned are bewailing their luck; they died suddenly (presumably before they could repent and confess in order to attain salvation). A devil, however, spells out the truth. Quevedo echoes a passage from Seneca here, and repeats some of these points in one of his most famous sonnets, 'Miré los muros de la patria mía' (*12*, p.31):

> Mentís — dijo un diablo—. Que ningún hombre muere de repente; y de descuidado y divertido, sí. ¿Cómo puede morir de repente quien dende que nace ve que va corriendo por la vida y lleva consigo la muerte? ¿Qué otra cosa oís en los púlpitos y leéis en los libros? ¿A qué volvéis los ojos, que no os acuerde de la muerte? Vuestro vestido que se gasta, la casa que se cae, el muro que se envejece y hasta el sueño cada día os acuerda de la muerte, retratándola en sí. (130)

Quevedo turns again from this sombre tone to satire on apothecaries, one of his favourite low satire targets, attacked again in *Muerte* and in the *Hora de todos*. He relates them to another target, alchemists, since they achieve the aim of alchemy, and turn base matter into gold, by their sale of base ingredients as medicine, for gold. Characteristically, Quevedo observes that they misuse words, and name ingredients falsely — 'y no compra sino palabras el que compra' (131). Some of these, we note with surprise, are saved from hell. He passes rapidly by barbers, left-handed people (thought to be evil portents at this time)[6] and women and their cosmetics, using some ancient insults dating at least from Martial, to arrive at one of the most memorable of the damned, viewed with horror by Quevedo. This sinner is suffering anguish, without being tormented by any visible demons. Quevedo can move with disconcerting speed from a comic and satirical hell of the seventeenth century to a very modern vision of hell, in the mind. This victim is being tormented by the good he could have done on earth; the three powers of the soul, the memory, the will, and the intelligence are still in action, as 'sayones incorpóreos' (134).

A little later Quevedo meets Judas Iscariot in hell. He is the first historical figure to appear in the *Sueño*, and he makes a speech in his own defence (he appeared briefly in *Juicio*, p.85). The device of allowing persons and personified phrases to defend themselves and satirize men while doing so is also used in *Muerte*, and in the *Discurso de todos los diablos* (*25, 28*). Quevedo now works out the significance of Judas more fully; the later *Sueños* frequently re-work material touched on in the first two. He begins with a joke about dishonest stewards of whom Judas is a kind of patron saint, or non-saint. He moves to obscene satire (Judas as a *capón*), and then, like a curious visitor to a prison, he addresses Judas directly. Judas forcefully points out, as he did in *Juicio*, that his betrayal was to the benefit of all Christians, and, not strictly a defence but a point for satire and moral teaching, that there are many worse than he:

> Y no penséis que soy yo solo el Judas, que después que Cristo murió hay otros peores que yo y más ingratos, pues no sólo le venden, pero le venden y compran, azotan y crucifican; y lo que es más que todo, ingratos a vida y pasión y muerte y resurrección, le maltratan y persiguen en nombre de hijos suyos. (136)

The tone of the whole passage is uneven, however; Quevedo uses

6 See Michèle Gendreau-Massaloux, 'Le Gaucher selon Quevedo: un homme à l'envers', in *L'Image du monde renversé* (see note 5 above), pp.73-89.

the associations and attributes of Judas to snipe at Jews, Portuguese, and Calabrians as well to make a moral point. We are soon to meet some of the people Judas describes as worse than himself.

After another break in the serious tone, to attack notaries, *alguaciles*, and prostitutes (one of whom offers a perverse defence to illustrate a reversed morality), Quevedo deals with sin by means of words. He was obsessed with the foolishness of apparently meaningless catch-phrases. Here we meet 'pensé que' as a foolish phrase which damned many lovers ('pensé que no me obligara, pensé que no me amartelara, pensé que ella me diera a mí y no me quitara'). The next section is about users of words and is more comic. Quevedo comes into the poets' corner of hell, where he finds a bad poet helpless before the demands of rhyme, and offers us an enjoyable example of his disastrous verse. He also jeers at the stock pastoral and jewellers' phrases of conventional poets; this is a topic found in one of his early mock-decrees on things which annoyed him (*10*, pp.67-68). He remembers his own sins in this respect and moves on, to a sombre passage on evilly-motivated prayer. 'Los que no supieron pedir a Dios' are silenced for their sin, and forced to listen to a vigorous sermon. This is satire of the high moral type; the sources are Lucian, Juvenal, Persius, and, no doubt, contemporary preaching. This demon reproaches the sinners in particularly positive terms:

> ¿Pedisteis alguna vez a Dios paz en el alma, aumento de gracia o favores suyos ni inspiraciones? No, por cierto; ni aun sabéis para qué son menester estas cosas ni lo que son. Ignoráis que el holocausto, sacrificio y oblación que Dios recibe de vosotros es de la pura conciencia, humilde espíritu, caridad ardiente. Y esto, acompañado con lágrimas, es moneda, que aun Dios, si puede, es cudicioso en nosotros. (143)

The devil works up to a reference to the Lord's Prayer, on which Quevedo wrote a devout commentary in *La cuna y la sepultura* (*10*, p.1092). From the darkness of hell this sermon on communication with God by means of words reaches out to the reader. Quevedo has not finished with words in hell; he concludes this section with 'ensalmadores ardiéndose vivos, y los saludadores también condenados por embustidores' (144). These were the quacks and faith-healers of the time; Quevedo sardonically notes the remoteness in place and time of their cures, and their use of solecisms, although he weakens the satire by admitting that some who loved God may been saved.

We now approach a section which is obscure to the modern reader. Quevedo is moving towards the area of the sinners who are worse than Judas, and on the way sees the quarters of the astrologers, geomancers, and alchemists. (This section has been studied by Martinengo (*30*), Mas (*31*), and Morreale (*32*).) Quevedo is apparently quite well-informed about alchemists, although he is totally sceptical about them here. He includes other satirical targets in this section; since it was one of the aims of alchemy to turn base matter into gold, tailors, constables, and alchemists themselves are clearly suitable for experiment. We observe that the alchemists and astrologers are still pursuing their researches in hell, and these researches are presumably what brought them there; we should also observe that they too are authors. Quevedo includes beautiful women among these 'autores, presos por hechiceros' — these are genuine sorcerers, satirized by means of metaphor.

Quevedo finally arrives at the place of sinners who are worse than Judas. They are the heretics, and are placed in an interior framework of allegory:

> A la puerta estaba la justicia de Dios, espantosa, y en la entrada, el vicio desvergonzado y soberbio, la malicia ingrata e ignorante, la incredulidad resuelta y ciega y la inobediencia bestial y desbocada. Estaba la blasfemia insolente y tirana llena de sangre, ladrando por cien bocas ... Grande horror me dio el umbral. (150)

The heretics who are listed, with some account of their absurd beliefs (the tone soon becomes comic), are safe satire for the amusement and incredulity of the contemporary reader.

Quevedo apparently took the names from a catalogue of heretics available to him.[7] The list continues until he meets Mohammed in hell and asks him some sarcastic anti-Muslim questions about alcohol and dietary rules. Mohammed does not defend himself, as some historical figures do in Quevedo's satire; he condemns himself and his followers by his reply. Quevedo also sees Luther, reproaches him (in the 1627 edition) and preaches to him on the question of images and works. Quevedo (rather than one of the devils) is preaching to one of the damned, and himself supplies Luther's side of the argument. The whole passage sounds odd in this satirically conceived hell, and the *Juguetes* version seems more appropriate. We may wonder, faced with this passage, how consistently Quevedo viewed his task in writing the *Sueños*; certainly serious, though rather obvious, religious debate and rough satire are rapidly and surprisingly juxtaposed.

Finally, in a separate gallery, Quevedo sees a number of historical figures, kings and emperors, with no Spanish representatives. They are only briefly mentioned here; they exchange recriminations in the *Discurso de todos los diablos*. He also sees a number of minor satirical targets, including *cornudos*, doctors, *doncellas hocicadas*, and constables. One other group is mentioned: 'muchos coronistas, lindas piezas, aduladores de molde y con licencia' (158). Writers of sycophantic history are also attacked in the *Discurso*; satire, as we have seen, interests itself in literature. Quevedo concludes conventionally, hoping that the reader, by reading, will avoid going to hell. With this defensive statement, and no elaborate procedure of awaking from a vision, he ends: 'Acabé este discurso en el Fresno, a postrero de abril de 1608, en 28 de mi edad.'

Despite its unevenness, this is one of the best of the *Sueños*. To some extent, it is a re-working, on a bigger scale, of *Juicio*. In *Muerte* there is a careful introduction, with emphasis on the fictional nature of the work, the description of the roads of life

---

[7] Maldonado (6, p.151), notes that the passage is not found in manuscript versions of the *Sueños*; it may have been added to the first edition. It was largely retained, although with some changes, in the 1631 (*Juguetes*) edition, which therefore authenticates it. Origen and Tertullian for instance are mentioned in 1627 but not in 1631.

(an idea he is to vary somewhat in the next *Sueño*), and then the great survey of the sad and comic variety of hell. To Quevedo moves rapidly and skilfully between trivial social satire and the sermons, preached by devils. The serious tone of the *Sueño* is first revealed by the tripartite sermon on honour, rank, and bravery, staples of the life of the *hidalgo*. To this class Quevedo himself belonged; he is as aware of its failings as he is of those of the despised tradesmen of Madrid. Quevedo invites his readers to read jokes about piemakers and then holds them for grim reminders about matters such as the vanity of social class, the opportunity to do good works, and true prayer. The principle of 'deleitar aprovechando' is at work, in fact. Revelation of the truth is one of the basic themes of the *Sueños*: in hell the devils can drop the deceits they use on earth, and sinners can reveal what they were. The minor sinners can be laughed at; the major sinners are tragic figures. The alchemists, astrologers, and heretics who conclude the *Sueño* misled men on earth in the past and the present. We cannot fail to observe in this *Sueño*, finally, Quevedo's interest in language, wordplay and wit, and also in the misuse of phrases, the wrong use of prayer, the sale of evil books. Much of the satire here is conventional and traditional, but it reveals Quevedo's moral attitude to the use of language. This *Sueño* also expresses its moral purpose in an interesting and unusual way; sermons from devils have more force than sermons from the clergy, and Quevedo is sharply aware of this (see *34*, pp.160-89). Quevedo plays his part as the eyewitness, the appalled or amused observer on our behalf. He is to play an even larger part in the fourth *Sueño*.

d) *El mundo por de dentro*

This is the *Sueño* most affected by changes in the 1631 edition. It was written in 1612 and dedicated to Quevedo's later patron, the Duque de Osuna. The first dedication refers only to Quevedo's desire for fame, in parody of the usual modest style of address, and to the greatness of the Duque. The 1631 version has the same date but is more conventional in tone: 'Estas burlas, que llevan en la risa disimulada algún miedo provechoso, envío para que vuecelencia se divierta de grandes ocupaciones ...' (*7*, vol.II, p.11). By 1631 Osuna was dead, and this version was intended in any case to be more respectable.

The address to the reader is in the flippant vein we now expect; the remarks which follow are sceptical of knowledge and of the possibility of anyone knowing anything. In the 1631 version a significant gesture to the religious censor is added: theologians, philosophers, and jurists are excepted — they are regarded as true students of the truth (*7*, vol.II, p.13). Quevedo goes comically through various kinds of ignorance coming finally to those who are totally sceptical about everything; these, who include himself, can print or publish all their dreams, and Quevedo looks for a moment at what happens to publication: 'se atreven a imprimir y sacar a luz todo cuanto sueñan. Estos dan que hacer a las emprentas, sustentan a los libreros, gastan a los curiosos, y al cabo, sirven a las especerías' (162). The conventional attitude was to hope that a book would go forth and have moral effects. Quevedo looks back briefly at the earlier *Sueños* (his only expression of a sense of them as a group is retrospective) and dismisses the reader, expressing contemptuous disregard for his opinion of the work he is about to read.

The narrative begins on a devotional and confessional note: Quevedo describes himself as a young man, a willing victim of the deceits of the world, quarrelsome, gluttonous, and confused. He is accosted by a ragged old man, who halts him by the force of his eloquence, and reproaches him for his foolish life.[8] In a moving speech, reminiscent of Quevedo's great poetry on the subject, he reminds him of the passage of time:

> ¿Tú, por ventura, sabes lo que vale un día? ¿Entiendes de cuánto precio es una hora? ¿Has examinado el valor del tiempo? Cierto que no, pues así, alegre, le dejas pasar, hurtado de la hora que, fugitiva y secreta, te lleva, preciosísimo robo. ... Sábete que la muerte y ellos están

---

[8] A.C. Spearing (*40*, p.10), following Macrobius, notes that in one kind of dream an authoritative and revered figure appears and gives information and advice. Quevedo uses this device again in *Muerte*.

eslabonados y en una cadena, y que, cuando más caminan
los días que van delante de ti, tiran hacia ti y te acercan a la
muerte, que quizá la aguardas y es ya llegada y, según
vives, antes será pasada que creída. (164)

The whole speech is in the best metaphorical style of the
seventeenth-century sermon. It moves Quevedo, and Desengaño
introduces himself. His clothes, torn by people who claim to
welcome disillusion, reveal what he is, in contrast to the figures
to come, whose dress conceals what they are. He invites
Quevedo to come with him to see the world as it really is, and
this is the central idea of the *Sueño*.

The allegorical manner continues; the main street of the world
is called Hypocrisy, and we have a sudden descent of style in the
first brief survey of hypocrites: false gentlemen, fake *discretos*,
old men who dye their beards, and the satirical commonplaces
about false naming we have seen earlier. A more serious note
returns with the idea that sin itself is hypocrisy. Desengaño
reminds Quevedo and the reader that according to Thomist
doctrine the will desires only the good; evil must therefore
disguise itself (hypocritically) as good in order to entice men to
sin; the point is graphically made by Gracián in the *Criticón* and
by Calderón in the *autos sacramentales*. *Desengaño* is an
essential prerequisite for religious as well as stoic belief. False
appearances are the great theme of this *Sueño*; this sombre
opening is more grave than the comic destruction of false
pretences we find in other *Sueños* and in some of Quevedo's
verse. Desengaño continues the attack upon hypocrisy, quoting
Job and declaring that hypocrisy is the gravest of sins: 'Todos
los pecadores tienen menos atrevimiento que el hipócrita, pues
ellos pecan contra Dios; pero no con Dios ni en Dios. Mas el
hipócrita peca contra Dios, y con Dios, pues le toma por instru-
mento para pecar' (168). A further passage, in which words of
Christ are quoted, was omitted in the 1631 edition, partly, no
doubt, because the religious censor would object to the divine in
a satire, and also perhaps because the moral and ethical aspects
of the discourse threaten the balance of the whole.

Quevedo and his mentor, presumably his older self, now see

the first of the spectacles on the street of hypocrisy: a funeral.[9] Firstly there is an already disabused description of the procession: the attendants are 'pícaros', the orphan children are 'meninos de la muerte' and 'lacayuelos del ataúd' and the clergy are 'galopando los responsos, cantaban de portante, abreviando, porque no se derritiesen las velas y tener tiempo para sumir a otro' (the disrespectful air of this description was attenuated for the 1631 edition). Quevedo's reaction is, despite this, decidedly naïve. The old man corrects him contemptuously, promising to show him the difference between appearances and reality. His corrections remind us of the devotional writing of the time: 'Allí va sino tierra de menos fruto y más espantosa de la que pisas, por sí no merecedora de alguna honra ni aun de ser cultivada con arado ni azadón' (170). Some of the critical remarks of Desengaño are cut and corrected in the 1631 edition (7, vol.II, p.29). The mourners are annoyed at having to attend and the widower is already thinking of another wife and regretting the expense of burying his first. Quevedo reacts for a second time to the funeral, in the light of what has been revealed to him, and he makes the final ascetic point:

> Quedé espantado de ver todo esto ser así, diciendo: —¡Qué diferentes son las cosas del mundo de como las vemos! Desde hoy perderán conmigo todo el crédito mis ojos y nada creeré menos de lo que viere.
>
> Pasó por nosotros el entierro, como si no hubiera de pasar por todos tan brevemente, yo como si aquella difunta no nos fuera enseñando el camino y, muda, no nos dijera a todos:
>
> Delante voy, donde aguardo a los que quedáis, acompañando a otros que yo vi pasar con ese propio descuido. (171)

The whole passage is an example of what Quevedo can achieve in the *Sueños* in satirical and ascetic writing.

The second scene in the street of hypocrisy is a widow's wake,

[9] Margherita Morreale notes that Lucian is a probable source of Quevedo here (*32*, p.219). Erasmus also criticizes elaborate funerals in *In Praise of Folly*.

or official mourning session, on the death of her husband. The initial description, before the reactions of Quevedo and Desengaño, is more obviously sardonic. When the women hear people coming, they strike up the appropriate wails in a room so dark they have to weep by touch. Despite this, Quevedo goes into a learned piece of rhetoric about the sympathy due to widows, with quotations from St Paul, Isaiah, and Job. It might well have seemed unacceptable to imitate the style of a learned sermon of the time in order, a few lines later, to deflate it ruthlessly, and so a long passage of Quevedo's pious and simple reaction is cut in the 1631 version. In both versions the old man reacts with contempt to Quevedo:

> ¿Ahora lloras, después de haber hecho ostentación vana de tus estudios y mostrádote docto y teólogo, cuando era menester mostrarte prudente? ¿No aguardaras a que yo te hubiere declarado estas cosas para ver cómo merecían que se hablare de ellas? (173)

The positive note here is prudence; we observe that studies and even theology can be misapplied; experience leading to *desengaño* is the best learning. We notice that the satirical target has been expanded, from hypocritical funerals to the man who is learned but cannot see things as they are.

The third scene is of an *alguacil* who has been wounded in pursuit of a criminal; a notary is also present. Again the scene is narrated with small touches of cynicism in advance of the expected revelation, and it seems that Quevedo as a narrator has learned nothing from the deceptions in the first two scenes. It is implied that the *alguacil* is drunk and that the notary is inventing or inflating the charges (a common satirical jibe).

Although we should not expect Quevedo to accept appearances in the case of either of these officials, he is acting here as the innocent observer, and so he again breaks into a panegyric and is again corrected by Desengaño, using points we have seen in previous *Sueños*. Desengaño somewhat deflates the attack by admitting that there may be some good *alguaciles*, but he concludes with a piece of connecting wit: 'Siento que cuando el

pregonero dice "A estos hombres por ladrones" que suene el eco
en la vara del alguacil y en la pluma del escribano' (176).

We note that the pace of the narrative is quickening, since
Quevedo is not allowed a second, chastened, reaction, as he was
in the earlier incidents. This shorter pattern is repeated in the
next section; the rich man in his carriage is a stiff and grotesque
figure, and his dignity is based upon credit. Quevedo enthuses
and Desengaño again deflates the appearance ('el mundo es sólo
trabajo y vanidad y éste es todo vanidad y locura'). He observes
that the rich man's buffoon and the rich man are laughing at
each other; sinners in the *Sueños* cooperate in life but not in
death.

A beautiful woman receives the same satirical treatment. She
is evidently a harlot on the look-out for custom ('iba ella con
artificioso descuido escondiendo el rostro a los que ya la habían
visto y descubriéndole a los que estaban divertidos', 178).
Quevedo, again as one might not expect, is overwhelmed and
wants to follow her, but is halted by the white hairs of
Desengaño, who advises him not to trust the evidence of his
senses:

> echo de ver que hasta ahora no sabes para lo que Dios te
> dio los ojos ni cuál es su oficio: ellos han de ver, y la razón
> ha de juzgar y elegir; al revés lo haces, o nada haces, que es
> peor. Si andas a creerlos, padecerás mil confusiones,
> tendrás las sierras por azules, y lo grande por pequeño, que
> la longitud y la proximidad engañan a la vista. (179)

He goes on to the traditional attack upon women and
cosmetics in organized style, with rhetorical questions, a listing
of the parts of the object attacked (hair, eyebrows, teeth, lips,
hands) and a series of sharp conditional sentences, ending on
indelicate physical detail (180).

In the first printed version of 1627 the *Mundo por de dentro*
ended here, and it is evidently without a proper conclusion (*6*,
pp.27-31). Quevedo apparently wrote the new ending for the
1631 edition, so the manuscript used for the 1627 *Sueños* may
well have been incomplete. The satirical device now used is that

of two giants who hold up a truth-revealing rope, under which different people pass, and are suddenly revealed for what they are. After the woman with whom the first version ended is exposed, we see a dignified-looking man revealed as a sponger; a lawyer, as a stirrer-up of litigation; a doctor, as a spreader of disease; a courtier, as one full of flattery and deceits; a cuckold and a false friend. The *cuerda* episode is thus a kind of satirical reprise which looks back to the rapid satirical survey of the opening passage of Desengaño's first speech to the narrator, and the fast changes of the earlier *Sueños*. Maldonado notes (*6*, p.29) that the sombre and dignified figure of the old man has been drastically changed; he is now senile and jeering. Just as the main body of *Dentro* anticipates an important satirical device of the *Criticón* of Gracián — a first naïve reaction to a person or situation, followed by a mature and disabused understanding — so the 'cuerda' passage anticipates the various devices of Gracián to detect the true nature of things. Quevedo extends the idea to his own writing as he concludes:

> hay debajo de la cuerda en todos los sentidos y potencias, y en todas partes y en todos oficios. Y yo lo veo por mí, que ahora escribo este discurso, diciendo que es para entretener, y por debajo de la cuerda doy un jabón muy bueno a los que prometí halagos muy sazonados. (184)[10]

Quevedo ends his narrative by falling asleep; after the nervous strain of these lessons of disillusion, he needs, as Desengaño advises, rest in order to digest them.

This is a *Sueño* of surprising variations of quality, as well as being a clear departure from the pattern set by the first three. The opening is in allegorical style; there is a swift satirical survey before we come to the main satirical revelations, which are more deliberate and thoughtful than the earlier *Sueños*. These central episodes are a contribution to the great contemporary theme of 'engaño a los ojos'; the final passage, written some seventeen

---

[10] The idea is repreated in different style in Quevedo's *La cuna y la sepultura*: 'Estas cosas son las que más te convienen y menos apacibles te parecen, y es menester a veces disfrazártelas, o con la elocuencia o variedad o agudeza, para que recibas salud del engaño' (*10*, p.1079).

years after the main part, is a tight piece of writing which returns to the rapid style of the *Sueños* in general.

e) *Sueño de la muerte* (*Visita de los chistes*)

Quevedo begins the last of the *Sueños* proper with a playful and affectionate note to an aristocratic lady, making fun of the usual commonplaces by means of wordplay, but also adding a formal note of intention: 'Procurado he pulir el estilo y sazonar la pluma con curiosidad; ni entre la risa me he olvidado de la doctrina' (184). We note however that this work was finished at a low point in Quevedo's career and life ('en la prisión y en la Torre, a 6 de abril, 1622'); he was under house arrest for his involvement in the affairs of the Duque de Osuna (see *11*, p.xxx). This may explain the complimentary references, to come, to the new king, Felipe IV; Quevedo was probably hoping to gain favour with the new regime. The short note to the reader is dismissive: there will be no more dreams; this is the last of the *Sueños* and its title is appropriate.

The opening is both sombre and powerful. Quevedo, in a state of melancholy and depression, is reading a stoical passage by Lucretius, welcoming death, and he quotes it to introduce his narrative. From the quotation his mind turns to a great figure of suffering, Job, whose book is three times quoted. (In the 1631 revision one of the quotations was replaced by a sonnet of anguished love which does not seem relevant; *7*, vol.I, p.199.) This *Sueño*, then, returns to the dream convention, inspired by reading books which reflect his state of mind. He falls asleep: 'luego que desembarazada el alma se vio ociosa sin la traba de los sentidos exteriores, me embistió desta manera la comedia siguiente, y así la recitaron mis potencias a escuras, siendo yo para mis fantasías auditorio y teatro' (188).[11] This reminds the reader of the remarks on dreams which opened *Juicio*, as well as of the conversation between Quevedo and his own disillusion. We should not, however, expect to find uncontrolled stream-of-consciousness writing in the *Sueños*; Quevedo is in command of

[11] A.C. Spearing refers to the relation between the author's state of mind, the books he is reading, and the dream he has, in the medieval tradition of dream literature (*40*, pp.55-56).

his material, and his *discurso* is to be varied and uneven, but not chaotic or surrealistic.

The narrative begins with a mysterious and ominous procession, a parody of the symbolic processions and triumphs which were public demonstrations of patriotism, religion, and power in this period. The passage describing doctors, apothecaries, surgeons, and tooth-pullers and talkers is a splendid example of Quevedo's satirical and deflating style (188-89); I consider this passage later in this Guide. The central figure of this comic and lethal procession is Death, who seems like a compound of all the attributes of death referred to by traditional ascetic writing. Quevedo is even amused by this vision until he realizes who she is and is invited to go with her on a visit of inspection of her kingdom. Death explains her entourage and herself to him and he takes on a traditional satirical role, that of the naïve, often uncomprehending, eye-witness and enquirer. She preaches to him, on the subject of death:

> La muerte no la conocéis, y sois vosotros mismos vuestra muerte. Tiene la cara de cada uno de vosotros, y todos sois muertes de vosotros mismos. La calavera es el muerto, y la cara es la muerte. Y lo que llamáis morir es acabar de morir, y lo que llamáis vivir es morir viviendo. (195)

She explains the company of medicals and talkers in satirical terms (we die of doctors and talkers rather than of diseases), and Quevedo indicates her function and her effect on him — 'la muerte predicadora y yo desengañado' — as the visit begins. The narrative moves from the satirical to the allegorical level. The world, the flesh, the devil, and money (worse than all three) guard the entrance. Judgement and Hell are found inside another door, and it is now Quevedo's turn to point a moral and link his vision with life on earth. He has seen hell before:

> en la codicia de los jueces, en el odio de los poderosos, en las lenguas de los maldicientes, en las malas intenciones, en las venganzas, en el apetito de los lujuriosos, en la vanidad

de los príncipes. Y donde cabe el infierno todo, sin que se pierda gota, es en la hipocresía de los mohatreros de las virtudes. (198)

The place of the tribunal of death is equally allegorical, with bad news, grief, envy, discord, and ingratitude all present. This scene is punctuated briefly by satire on tailors and marriage-brokers before returning to a fine allegorical-satirical passage on kinds of death ('la muerte de amores, la muerte de frío, la muerte de hambre, la muerte de miedo, y la muerte de risa'). These different deaths are satirical comments upon people who so die: tyrants and misers die of fear of revolution and robbery, for instance. 'La muerte de risa' is an anticipation of Quevedo's didactic exploitation of the *chistes* to follow; it applies to people who mock their opportunities to repent and reform in time, who cannot believe that they are dead when they are. Quevedo accepts the lesson; he will try to live well if he returns to life. Death now calls an assembly, and the *chistes* section of this *Sueño* begins. Quevedo is approached by personified catchphrases in the kingdom of death. As we have seen (p.31) he was interested in and annoyed by the worn-out phrases in common use at this time. The elaborate and powerful introduction is thus a preparation for the personification and the furiously defensive statements of such phrases, made into a formidably angry figure. The significance of the *habladores* in the procession becomes clear, and, although it seems a curious slackening of tension to turn to the satire of things as transient as common clichés and slang phrases, we should remember the importance attached to language in this age (see pp.74-75).

The defences made by the *chistes* turn into satire of the moral life of the time. 'Juan de la Encina' is the first to appear. His name was associated with *disparates*;[12] he responds furiously that all men do and say silly things, and he shifts his defence to moral attack:

[12] For Juan de la Encina and his *disparates*, see 7, vol.I, p.223n, and R.O. Jones, 'Juan del Encina and Posterity', in *Medieval Hispanic Studies presented to Rita Hamilton*, edited by A.D. Deyermond (London: Tamesis, 1976), pp.99-106.

¿Pudríme de que otro fuese rico o medrase? ¿He creído las
apariencias de la fortuna? ¿Tuve yo por dichosos a los que
al lado de los príncipes dan toda la vida por una hora?
(203)

His speech turns towards satire on doctors and social
observances, but points against envy and ambition have been
powerfully made.

Another phrase appears, 'el rey que rabió', apparently a
phrase meaning 'ancient and outmoded'. He is a kingly figure,
standing on his rank, as Quevedo observes, and he makes one
remark about the unhappy position of kings, surrounded by
flatterers, which reminds us that Quevedo was also the author of
the *Política de Dios*. The next *chiste* is also a proverbial king, 'el
rey Perico', whom Quevedo uses for the assertion, characteristic
of him as a conservative satirist, that past times were better than
the present. Anything old, outmoded, and dirty was from the
'tiempo del rey Perico', but virtue and good manners were also a
feature of the old times:

> Si un padre dice a un hijo: 'No jures, no juegues, reza las
> oraciones cada mañana, persígnate en levantándote, echa
> la bendición a la mesa' dice que 'eso se usaba en tiempo del
> rey Perico', y que ahora le tendrán por un maricón si sabe
> persignarse, y se reirán de él si no jura y blasfema. (205)

Quevedo is playing a double game here; he is condemning these
phrases as outmoded, while at the same time showing that they
have or can have real significance, that is, that they are still
alive.

In the next section he again uses a figure from the past to
comment upon the present. There was a popular legend that the
medieval nobleman, the learned Enrique de Villena, had bottled
and preserved himself in order to survive death.[13] Quevedo finds
his flask and in it the Marquis, who reconstitutes himself and
questions Quevedo about the present (of 1621) before he decides

[13] Villena (1384-1434) is generally, though inaccurately, known to posterity as
the Marqués de Villena, and it is in this way that Quevedo refers to him.

to return to life. The Marquis is another example of the revered and authoritative figure who appears in dreams and gives information and advice to the narrator (*40*, p.10). Quevedo is thus a witness here of the upper world, as the constabled devil in *Alguacil* was of the lower world. The Marquis's questions and Quevedo's answers are satire, mixed with flattery as we shall see, on the present. He first enquires whether there is peace in the world and is annoyed to hear that there is; he refuses to come out until reassured by Quevedo. War, according to some theorists, was a healthy and honourable state for a nation (since it was thought to encourage social discipline, bravery, and trust in God). The question must be related to the political debate in Madrid in 1621-22 as to whether the twelve years of peace with the Netherlands should be renewed (see *2*, pp.320-21; war was finally and disastrously decided upon). Quevedo is evidently in favour of war here; he was a natural conservative, and it seems likely that he is trying to ingratiate himself with the new king and his favourite, Olivares. The passage does not appear in the *Juguetes* version. The Marquis also enquires about the repute of money and of the Genoese, and Quevedo is able to satirize the power of both. The same device is used to attack *honra*, although not at the length or with the effectiveness of the sermon in *Infierno*. One detail about the present decadence of Spaniards is reminiscent or anticipatory of a passage of Quevedo's *Epístola satírica y censoria* (*12*, p.140, line 100). The Marquis is aware that Spaniards are now drinkers, whereas they were once famous for sobriety. The two go on to satirize cuckolds and lawyers; there is a vivid picture of an officious and venal lawyer, a sketch to be worked over again in the *Hora de todos*. After an attack on the Venetians, enemies of Spain in Italy (where Quevedo had served with the Duque de Osuna), and on courtiership, the Marquis asks who is the present king of Spain. When he hears that it is Felipe IV, he is pleased: 'más justicia se ha de hacer ahora por un cuarto que en otros tiempos por doce millones' (215). The remark reflects the optimism with which the new king was received, as well as some implied criticism of the venality and corruption of the reign of Felipe III, of which Quevedo had had direct experience.

After meetings with some minor *chistes*, of more interest to
the seventeenth-century reader than to us, Quevedo meets an old
man who is reminiscent of the figure of Desengaño in *El mundo
por de dentro*. This is 'Pedro' (or 'Pero') 'Grullo', the author of
nonsense prophecies and boring commonplaces, in doggerel
verse. (A *perogrullada* is a truism or platitude.) Quevedo again
takes up his double stance: he is annoyed by this worn-out
doggerel of inanities, but, on the other hand, all words have
some meaning, and he reads into these verses an ominous or
moral or satirical meaning. For instance:

Vosotros decís que mis profecías son disparates, y hacéis
mucha burla de ellas. Estemos a cuentas. Las profecías de
Pero Grullo, que soy yo, dicen así:
    Muchas cosas nos dejaron
    las antiguas profecías;
    dijeron que en nuestros días
    será lo que Dios quisiere.
Pues, bribones, adormecidos en maldad, infames, si esta
profecía se cumpliera, ¿había más que desear? Si fuera lo
que Dios quisiere, fuera siempre lo justo, lo bueno, lo
santo; no fuera lo que quiere el diablo, el dinero y la
cudicia. (217)

He goes on, this technique being established, to make a bitter
point about the acceptability of the truth: 'Diréis que de puro
verdad es necedad; ¡buen achaquito, hermanos vivos! La
verdad, ansí, decís que amarga; poca verdad decís que es
mentira; muchas verdades, que es necedad. ¿De qué manera ha
de ser la verdad para que os agrade?' (218). He goes on to attack
venal cuckolds, luxury goods, dubious parentage, notaries, and
the Genoese, to end, however, with some doggerel evidently
flattering to the new king. In this *Sueño* satire and some
personal purposes evidently come together.

Quevedo next attacks the habit of using clichés of lazy non-
specific (or even fictional) reference, to 'cierto autor' and 'no sé
quién' for instance, and some minor phrases, before changing
over to another narrative device, the set-piece description and

the defensive and offensive speeches of a single legendary or mythical figure. The first of these is the prototype and epitome of old women, the 'Dueña Quintañona'; the pungent description of her (223) reminds the reader of the treatment of figures such as the *licenciado* Calabrés, of *Alguacil*. As we observe the cruelty of the description, we should remember that the seventeenth century had its own sensibility; Quevedo has a number of poems in similar style. This old woman was a *dueña* in life, and she embarks upon an embittered and resentful description of *dueñas*. Quevedo does not reveal deep sympathy in her speech, but there is an awareness of the unhappy position of these women, who lived in a vague area between distrusted servants, alleged go-betweens, and family; this *dueña* at least would rather stay dead than return to her past life. She merely asks that the living cease from bandying her about from mouth to mouth. The whole passage is a sudden vivid glimpse of the social scene, of bullying and wasted lives.

The next set piece concerns a figure who represents the eternal sponger, 'el malcosido y peor sustentado don Diego de Noche'. Quevedo addresses him in joyful and mocking apostrophes: '¡Oh estómago aventurero! ¡Oh, gaznate de rapiña! ¡Oh, panza al trote!' (227). Don Diego asks for compassion, however; he describes his methods of disguising his poverty (the figure of the *caballero chanflón* is also found in the *Buscón* and in the *Hora de todos*). He describes some of the meaningless phrases directed at him in life; and the devils themselves are afraid he will sponge on them in death. Quevedo consigns other worn-out phrases to the kingdom of the dead by alluding to them here. When he meets Doña Fáfula or Fábula (*8*, p.275) he takes the opportunity to snipe at the clichés and stock situations of the current theatre, noting, for instance, the custom of marrying off all the characters at the end, and, in the poorer sort of *auto sacramental*, the fact that the devil, evidently a more exciting and melodramatic figure than the suffering Christ, gets the big part. Other catchphrases follow, most of which must have seemed funnier or more annoying to the contemporary reader; one or two stand out in a moment of seriousness or of satire directed at the world of the living. Quevedo meets a lost soul, 'el alma de Garibay', who comments upon the implications of his saying:

> habéis introducido decir que el alma de Garibay no la
> quiso Dios ni el diablo. Y en esto decís una mentira y una
> herejía. La herejía es decir que no la quiso Dios: que Dios
> todas las almas quiere y por todas murió. ... La mentira
> consiste en decir que no la quiso el diablo. ¿Hay alma que
> no la quiera el diablo? No por cierto. Que, pues él no hace
> asco de las de los pasteleros, roperos, sastres ni
> sombrereros, no lo hará de mí. (233)

There is a chilling awareness of the aims of the devil, even though the passage turns to the usual satire against the tradesmen. He exits, pursued by soul-less bodies all trying to catch him. There seems to be some confession of authorial fatigue here — 'estaba tal con la variedad de cosas que había visto, que no me acordaba de nada' (234), and some evidence of revision and censorship (236n). For a number of the phrases he meets we need the help of Correas and Covarrubias;[14] one or two however, like 'Juan de Buen Alma' (240) and 'la gata de Juan Ramos', have the characteristic social sting. 'La gata de Juan Ramos cierra los ojos y abre las manos' becomes an attack upon the corruption of society:

> Y lo peor de todo es que ahora no hay doncellita, ni conta-
> dorcito (que ayer no tenía que contar sino duelos y
> quebrantos), ni secretario, ni ministro, ni hipócrita, ni
> pretendiente, ni juez, ni pleiteante, ni viuda, que no se
> haga la gata de Juan Ramos. (243)

The final figure of the series is 'don Diego Moreno, un muerto de buena disposición, bien vestido y de buena cara', a prosperous *cornudo*. He makes a brazen defence of his way of life, and Quevedo threatens to return to the world to write

14 Gonzalo Correas, *Vocabulario de refranes y frases proverbiales*, edited by L.
Combet (Bordeaux: Féret, 1967), and Sebastián de Covarrubias Orozco, *Tesoro
de la lengua castellana o española* (1611), edited by Martín de Riquer (Barcelona:
Horta, 1943).

entremeses satirizing him. This is the first time Quevedo threatens any inhabitant of the kingdom of death with punishment in the upper world; there is some in-group humour here: an *entremés* on Don Diego by Quevedo has been rediscovered in modern times. (Quevedo also wrote an *entremés* entitled *Los refranes del viexo celoso* (*11*, p.555) in which the *refranes* used by an old man come as characters to tease him.) Quevedo and don Diego begin to fight and Quevedo wakes up:

> Con todo esto, me pareció no despreciar del todo esta visión y darle algún crédito, pareciéndome que los muertos pocas veces se burlan y que, gente sin pretensión y desengañado, más atiende a enseñar que a entretener. (243)

Quevedo thus ends the last of the *Sueños* on a note of teaching rather than entertainment. It may seem curious that after the sombre opening and the powerful appearance of death this *Sueño* should turn to attack on worn-out phrases. Language, however, is important to Quevedo, as it is to most satirists; and no language is entirely meaningless. *Perogrulladas* and *disparates* can have a profound moral significance.

f) A note on the *Discurso de todos los diablos* and the *Hora de todos*.

Quevedo published in the *Juguetes de la niñez* a satirical work entitled *El entremetido, la dueña y el soplón*; this was first published separately with the title *Discurso de todos los diablos, o infierno enmendado* in 1629 (*11*, p.1378). The bibliographical details are, as usual, complex, but it is evidently not one of the *Sueños*, although it is in their style, and at times uses material which might have been included in the third and fifth. The *Discurso* is preceded by the disrespectful preliminaries we expect, and the main device, with no reference to Quevedo (although the first person singular is occasionally used), is that of Lucifer and his staff going on a tour of hell, in the company of the busybody, the *dueña*, and the police informer. One feature only hinted at in the *Sueños* soon emerges: the party meets historical figures, like Julius Caesar, Alexander, and Tiberius, and their ministers or favourites, as well as certain classical historians and writers of political theory. These take the opportunity for self-justification and mutual recrimination. Alongside these political and historical passages, which reflect perhaps some of Quevedo's reading for the *Política de Dios*, are satirical passages on targets similar to those attacked in the *Sueños*: the tradesmen, knaves and fools, the deadly catch-phrases whose meaning is cruelly revealed. There is a strong political air about the *Discurso*, and less of a purely moral note than we find in the *Sueños*. There is some good satire on bribery, the law of precedent, honour, and ill-informed political comment. Lucifer concludes the visit with a perverse discourse advocating 'buena dicha' and 'prosperidad' as means to the corruption and damnation of men and society. Interestingly, some American imports, such as tobacco and chocolate, are attacked as dangerous and decadent novelties, and war is warned against by Lucifer, since it is a social purgative. Although there is less brilliance of style and less ferocious satire in the *Discurso* than in the *Sueños*, there is some air of wider horizons (see *34*, pp.39-46 for a good critical account of the *Discurso*).

Quevedo's greatest satirical work in prose, *La hora de todos y la fortuna con seso* reaches out to the widest range of satirical comment and confines moral comment to its outer framework. The satirical device is the decision by Jupiter, after a burlesqued council of the gods, to compel the pagan and truculent goddess, Fortune, to allow men on earth for a short while to have what they deserve, and not suffer her random dictates. The day and time are chosen and Quevedo describes fifty instances of injustice suddenly turned into justice. A number of satirical topics of the *Sueños* are found here: doctors, law officers, apothecaries, talkers, *dueñas*, tavern-keepers, alchemists, women, cosmetics, and coaches; these sections seem to be Quevedo's final working-over of the well-known objects of his low satire. He extends his range of satirical commentary considerably, however, to make political comments on internal and external affairs, taking in most of the known world and subjects such as taxation, economics, law, the system of royal favourites, international banking, and a chaotic meeting of disunited nations. Jupiter pessimistically concludes that things are no better when justice is imposed upon the world, and instructs Fortune to return to her old random ways; what we call Fortune is only the providence of God, wrongly understood.

3. Style and Structure

Aspects of the style and structure of the *Sueños* have necessarily been referred to in the account of each one. I now recapitulate to some extent, but it is useful to consider structure and style apart from themes, in order to see what Quevedo brought to his largely conventional material in the *Sueños*.

a) Dedications and preliminary notes

The preliminaries to seventeenth-century works are rarely meaningless (Cervantes's prologues, for instance, are usually important, even when ambiguous). The general prologue to the 1627 *Sueños* was apparently written by Juan Sapera; it prepares the reader for satire, wit, and moral lessons, and it is an interesting indication of how an evidently experienced contemporary looked at the *Sueños*. It is replaced in 1631 by rather defensive notes, by Quevedo and his editor, Messia de Leiva, which do however refer to wit and teaching. The individual dedications to separate *Sueños* are generally straightforward. The notes to the reader, whether prologues or notes, help to set the atmosphere; when they are serious or semi-serious, they point to the moral purpose of the discourses to follow; when they are comic in tone, they contribute to the air of parody and disrespect, and are part of the entertainment.

b) Openings; dream convention; endings

Each of the narratives sets up a situation which is a satirical device. These are: a dream, inspired by devotional literature; a visit to a priest and a madman in a church; a vision of two roads of life, and the hell one road leads to; another vision, of a survey of the main street of life, with an interpreter; a final dream of a visit to the kingdom of death. These scene-setting devices become more elaborate, the longest being also the last, in

Muerte. A number of features of the medieval dream poem noted in A.C. Spearing's book are clearly applicable here (*40*, pp.1-18, are particularly relevant). Spearing refers, among other features, to: the classical and Christian traditions of the significance of dreams (see *Juicio* and *Muerte*); the *oraculum* type of dream, in which an authoritative figure visits the writer or narrator (see *Dentro* and *Muerte*); the presence of the writer in the dream, as himself or as another (see below); the idea that dreams are caused by the mental state of the dreamer, the books he happens, or chooses, to read, and his waking preoccupations (see *Juicio* and *Muerte*); the beginnings of dreams or visions in an idyllic pastoral place (*Infierno*); and the independence afforded to a work of literary art by the use of the dream convention. Quevedo is not exploiting this tradition with the subtlety and profundity of a Chaucer or a Langland, but he is evidently indebted to it. He uses aspects of the dream-convention as a protection for his satire, no doubt, and also probably because it permitted him a chaotic and comic narrative style, appropriate to dreams and traditional to satire.

Whereas the beginnings of the individual *Sueños* are careful and calculated, the endings are surprisingly cursory; Quevedo merely wakes up and points briefly to a moral, or he suddenly turns to his patron in the hope that he will learn the lesson, or he retreats into defensive statements about non-specific satire. We deduce that for Quevedo the dream convention was not much more than a known satirical device.

c) 'Yo'; different speakers

Spearing also points to the importance of the poet in medieval dream poems (*40*, pp.5-6, 19, 68), although he may at times be absent in the course of the narration. Quevedo is present in the preliminaries to the *Sueños* as a person who needs protection and patronage; he addresses the reader as a writer and as a satirist of conventional writing, and he takes part in the narrations as 'yo', a persona of the writer. 'Yo' is sometimes merely an appalled or amused eyewitness; sometimes he refers to himself in the narrations as a poet or as a lover; he occasionally

meets in hell acquaintances from his own life. The three
Quevedos are therefore sometimes hard to separate, since he was
a poet and presumably was a lover, and since he occasionally
moves (as at the end of *Juicio* and *Infierno*) from the narrator to
the real person. Obviously, what 'yo' sees is selected by
Quevedo, the writer, and so we might deduce, to some extent,
which aspects of society and moral life preoccupied the real
Quevedo (bearing in mind, however, that many of Quevedo's
satirical topics are also found in traditional satire). Quevedo also
uses the narrating 'yo' to invite or guide a reaction in the reader;
he laughs at trivial or comic sinners, but he turns away in horror
before more serious and anguished cases, sometimes relating the
sin to himself. 'Yo' also takes an active part in the proceedings
(after *Juicio*, where he is only an eyewitness who laughs or is
awed). He asks questions of the damned or of the devils;
occasionally (as to Luther, Judas, and Muerte) he makes moral
pronouncements himself. In *Alguacil* he asks questions of the
devil and so guides and selects the account of hell. In *Dentro* he
plays a vital part, standing for the naïve reader, as well as for his
own older and disillusioned self; he describes the scene and
reacts both incorrectly and correctly to it. In *Muerte* he is an eye-
witness, a preacher, and an interrogator; he talks with the *chistes*
and the figures, and ponders over their replies. He steps back,
however, in some passages, and varies the narrative with other
speakers, most notably the devils, who explain, mock, preach
(to the narrator, the damned, and the reader), and even tell the
truth.

d) Internal organization

Within the frameworks of dream and vision, the narratives
have little formal structure; the satirical points, characters, or
scenes follow each other without any apparent organization.
(Only in *Infierno* do we have some sense of moving deeper into
hell.) The moral and satirical elements interrupt each other,
sometimes disconcertingly. The main satirical idea is that people
are placed in circumstances which expose their past or present
falsity, their sin, their remorse (or brazen lack of it). Their

situations, comic or dreadful, are to amuse and to be a lesson to the reader. Some of the humour is based upon the idea that their ruling passions survive death and are still active in hell. In two of the *Sueños* (*Dentro* and *Muerte*) allegory, one of the traditional devices of satire, is employed.

There is no attempt to impose narrative organization by any use of location. In *Juicio* there is a movement towards the scene of God sitting in judgement, but there is no placing of sinners in any order; people come on in disorderly procession and are lost from sight. The devil in *Alguacil* is guided by Quevedo's questions and interests to some extent, but he reveals that the sinners in hell are grouped by senses of words if anything. In *Infierno*, Quevedo wanders about hell giving only vague topographical references — 'subíme por una cuesta', 'entréme por un corral adelante'. In *Mundo* we have unity of place, in that we visit the street of hypocrisy. The structure, however, consists of an introductory section of false appearances, the main sections of appearance, reaction, and revelation, and a kind of coda which is akin to the introduction, although this section seems rather tacked on. In *Muerte* we have the great procession culminating in the arrival and the invitation of Death, but when Quevedo goes with her to visit her kingdom, the narrative returns to the loose structure of *Juicio* and *Infierno*; various *chistes* and types come to talk to Quevedo. The first, third, and fifth *Sueños* are similar in structure, being eyewitness accounts; the second and fourth describe Quevedo with a reporter or a guide. The *Discurso* is closer to *Juicio*, *Infierno* and *Muerte* than to the other two. In the *Hora de todos* Quevedo found a comparatively simple structure which enables him to achieve a huge panorama of satire with unity of time. The loose narrative structures of the *Sueños* are common to traditional satire; they permit variety of episodes and radical changes of tone, but also reveal some casualness of approach. Loose structures have advantages and disadvantages: the Marqués de Villena episode enlivens *Muerte*, but the passage about alchemists, astrologers, and heretics prolongs *Infierno* unnecessarily. (For a detailed account of the structural devices of the *Sueños*, see *34*, ch.2.)

e) Set pieces; development of satirical material

The *Sueños* are punctuated by set-piece passages of great force. A celebrated example is the description of the *licenciado* Calabrés in *Alguacil*, which has been compared with that of the 'dómine Cabra' in *La vida del buscón*. Other examples are the Dueña Quintañona and Don Diego de Noche in *Muerte*, as well as the highly allegorical account of Death itself. The first account of the sights seen by Quevedo and Desengaño in *Dentro* are also set pieces, which are then analysed by the two. Probably the greatest set piece in the *Sueños* is the procession of the agents of death in *Muerte*.

Another feature of the *Sueños*, seen as a whole, is the re-working of satirical material; we have observed that *Juicio* contains short references to a number of topics which are expanded later. For example, the treatment of the figure of Judas Iscariot, or of law officers, or the misuse of clichés, can be compared from one *sueño* to another. It is possible to examine both these features of style together in the description of the entourage of death in *Muerte*; this passage also shows in action and in context some aspects of Quevedo's verbal style to which I refer later.

The most conspicuous agents of death are doctors and apothecaries, usually found close to each other. In *Juicio* there is an early brief treatment:

Ante este doctor han pasado los más difuntos, con ayuda de este boticario y barbero; y a ellos se les debe gran parte de este día. Alegó un ángel por el boticario que daba de balde a los pobres medicinas; pero dijo un diablo que hallaba por su cuenta que habían sido más dañosos dos botes de su tienda que diez mil de pica en la guerra, porque todas sus medicinas eran espurias, y que con esto había hecho liga con una peste y había destruido dos lugares. (82)

We note that some *boticarios* are saved, and that there is a pun on 'bote' ('thrust', 'medicine jar').

Quevedo returns to *boticarios* in *Infierno* (130-31) where he mentions their ability to create gold out of base materials and their use of words to deceive the patient about the true nature of their prescriptions. He uses here the metaphor he is to use in *Muerte*:

> Y su nombre no había de ser boticarios sino armeros; ni sus tiendas no se habían de llamar boticas, sino armerías de los doctores, donde el médico toma la daga de los lamedores, el montante de los jarabes y el mosquete de la purga maldita, demasiada, recetada a mala sazón y sin tiempo. (131)

There is a short attack on the appearance and the reality of a doctor in *Dentro*; under the revealing *cuerda* he appears as a lethal cavalryman:

> Mira aquel que fuera de la cuerda viste a la brida en mula tartamuda de paso, con ropilla y ferreruelo y guantes y receta, dando jarabes, cuál anda aquí a la brida en un basilisco, con peto y espaldar y con manoplas, repartiendo puñaladas de tabardillos, y conquistando las vidas, que allí parecía que curaba. Aquí por debajo de la cuerda está estirando las enfermedades para que den de sí y se alarguen, y allí parecía que rehusaba las pagas de las visitas. (182)

The rapid changes from what he is to what he seems are very effective. Quevedo's longest and most detailed treatment of these colleagues is the set-piece at the beginning of *Muerte*:

> Fueron entrando unos médicos a caballo en unas mulas, que con gualdrapas negras parecían tumbas con orejas. El paso era divertido y torpe, de manera que los dueños iban encima en mareta y algunos vaivenes de serradores. (188)

Doctors travelled on mules; with their black trappings these inspire the metaphor 'tumbas con orejas' — an anticipation of the effect of the doctor's visit. They rarely hurry and they sway from side to side like sawyers at work (there is a hint of 'sawbones' here). The verbal and witty elements are conspicuous:

> la vista asquerosa de puro pasear por orinales y servicios; las bocas emboscadas en barbas, que apenas se las hallara un braco; sayos con resabios de vaqueros; guantes en infusión, doblados como los que curan; sortijón en el pulgar con piedra tan grande que cuando toma el pulso pronostica al enfermo la losa. (189)

Their sight is imagined as contaminated with the vessels they examine for diagnosis; the connection of ideas is daring, almost surrealistic, and nauseating. Their mouths are hidden in their beards as if lying in ambush; their smocks are those of cowmen rather than scientists; 'guantes doblados' can refer to folded gloves, or, with 'como los que curan', to patients doubled-up with pain; Maldonado (6) notes the complexity of 'en infusión' (189). Doctors wore rings with stones thought to have curative properties; Quevedo wittily connects their stones to gravestones.

The doctors are accompanied by assistants and pupils who learn medicine by looking after the mules; Quevedo connects their learning and its effects: 'Si de éstos se hacen estos otros [doctors from 'platicantes'], no es mucho que estos otros nos deshagan a nosotros' (189). There is a deadly play between 'hacen' and 'deshagan'. Quevedo now turns to apothecaries, using the military analogy of drawn weapons we saw in *Infierno*: 'Alrededor venía gran chusma y caterva de boticarios con espátulas desenvainadas y jeringas en ristre, armados de cala en parche, como de punta en blanco' (189). 'Chusma' and 'caterva' are contemptuous; they look like deadly soldiers. Their ancient and deteriorated medicines are in flasks and they issue them for gain — 'así son medecinas redomadas las suyas'. There is wordplay, as Maldonado explains, between 'redomas' (flasks) and 'redomadas', which means 'mean and crafty'. Quevedo moves on to the chilling and imaginative connection of disease, treatment, and death: 'El clamor del que muere empieza en el almirez del boticario, va al pasacalles del barbero, paséase por el tableteado de los guantes del doctor, y acábase en las campanas de la iglesia' (189). One mortal sound leads to another (barbers, who also bled people, were apparently given to playing guitars in idle moments, 131): the dying man's groans, the grind of the pestle, the incongruous guitar, the tapping of the deadly glove, the bell tolling for the dead.

Quevedo goes on with his military metaphor and applies it to the attributes of *boticarios*:

> No hay cosa suya que no tenga achaques de guerra y que no aluda a armas defensivas. Jarabes que antes sobran letras para jara, que les falten. Botas que se dicen los de pica, espátulas son espadas en su lengua, píldoras son balas ... (190)

Jargon is employed to develop the metaphor. Quevedo rapidly changes to another metaphor, by means of wordplay: 'si así se toca la tecla de las purgas, sus tiendas son purgatorios, y ellos los infiernos, los enfermos los condenados, y los médicos los diablos' (the wordplay 'purga/purgatorios' can easily be missed). The metaphor 'diablos/doctores' required explanation: 'Y es cierto que son diablos los médicos, pues unos y otros andan tras los malos y huyen de los buenos, y todo su fin es que los buenos sean malos y que los malos no sean buenos jamás' (190). The play on the senses of 'buenos' and 'malos' is obvious. Quevedo moves from what the apothecaries are allegedly wearing, to their language and professional jargon:

> Venían todos vestidos de recetas y coronados de reales erres asaetados, con que empiezan las recetas. Y consideré que los dotores hablan a los boticarios diciendo 'Recipe' que quiere decir recibe. De la misma suerte habla la mala madre a la hija, y la codicia al mal ministro. (190)

From the conventional crossed capital Rs with which prescriptions began (Quevedo's interest in language extends to technical writing), he moves to a sudden attack on the venality of women and of ministers. In the lines that follow he returns to the crossed Rs, alludes to the Santa Hermandad which killed criminals with arrows, and moves to wordplay again:

> ¡Pues decir que en la receta hay otra cosa que erres asaetadas por delincuentes, y luego ana, ana, que juntas hacen un Annas para condenar a un justo! Síguense uncias y más onzas: ¡qué alivio para desollar un cordero enfermo! (190)

Maldonado explains that 'ana' is a unit of measurement; this becomes 'Annas' and the 'justo' refers to the patient, as well as to Christ. This echoes into the play of 'ounces' (cats and weights) and the 'cordero enfermo'. We may feel that Quevedo is being carried away by his own wit here. He gives a list of the technical terms for the ingredients they use, and the prosaic things these ingredients really are; deceit is made possible by words. Both the names and the things they represent have the effect of repelling the diseases, by nausea rather than by appropriateness (191). Quevedo is accusing the apothecaries of false naming, mystification, and being worse than the diseases. He returns to the doctors, and in an attack on their methods of diagnosis, he personifies the faeces:

> van al servicio y al orinal a preguntar a los meados lo que no saben, porque Galeno les remitió a la cámara y a la orina. Y como si el orinal les hablase al oído, se le llegan a la oreja, avahándose los barbones con su niebla. ¿Pues, verles hacer que se entienden con la cámara por señas, y tomar su parecer al bacín, y su dicho a la hedentina? (191)

The subject of 'saben' may be either doctors or 'los meados'; the contemptuous reference to the authority of Galen is also note-worthy; times were changing.

Quevedo ends his denunciation with the rhetorical device of a string of verbs, a device he uses a few lines later to attack the surgeons in the cavalcade: 'ahorcan con el garrotillo, degüellan con sangrías, azotan con ventosas, destierran las almas, pues las sacan de la tierra de sus cuerpos sin alma y sin conciencia!'

(191). In this long set-piece passage, before we arrive at the figure of death and begin the visit to her kingdom, Quevedo uses wordplay; puns; the relationship between words and things; metaphor, and derived metaphor, sometimes explained; wit and rapid connection of ideas; wide allusion, sometimes turning away from the particular satirical target; rhetoric; and base allusion.

f) Sermons and discourses

One of the great features of the *Sueños* is the vigorous style of the moral and satirical discourses and sermons which punctuate the narratives (there are ten such discourses in *Infierno* alone). The devils preach forcefully as part of the punishment of the damned, and for the benefit of the reader. Quevedo is aware that a sermon from a devil would probably be more interesting than one from a saint, although he is also aware that devils are usually liars. When they preach recognizable morality, we presume that they are telling the truth. These rather ambiguous preachers use the rhetorical devices of the sermons of the time. In the great attack on nobility, honour, and bravery in *Infierno*, there are command forms, examples from history, contemptuous diminutives ('toda la sangre, hidalguillo, es colorada'), enumeration of headings, rhetorical questions, repetition of phrases ('por la honra ... por la honra'), and descent into rough but coarsely effective language: 'La honra está junto al culo de las mujeres; la vida en manos de los doctores, y la hacienda, en las plumas de los escribanos: ¡desvaneceos, pues, bien mortales!' (124). We can hardly imagine a conventional preacher using such language then, or even now. Elsewhere, Quevedo uses sequences of rhetorical questions (129, the passage on 'nadie muere de repente'), he relates the discourse to seventeenth-century psychology (133), he attacks the hearer to wake him up (217), he anticipates the reader's reaction (218), and he supplies the reaction himself. He can be cautious about preaching, however; when he runs up a compassionate and learned discourse on the subject of widows (172), Desengaño deflates it with a counter-sermon on prudence.

Learning, Biblical allusion, rhetoric and easy emotional
responses are not enough. As we read these energetic moral
pronouncements, we remember that the most effective sections
of a devotional work like *La cuna y la sepultura* are the attacks
upon the vanity and the presumptions of men rather than the
exhortations of the latter part, however eloquent. Quevedo
makes the most of the paradoxical and perverse contexts offered
to him by his visions; unexpected preachers pronounce with
energy and skill. Rapid movement from serious discourse to
flippant satire full of pun and allusion is a chief feature of the
Sueños.

g) Verbal level

The verbal style of Quevedo in word, phrase, and sentence has
attracted considerable scholarly attention, especially with regard
to his poetry and the *Buscón*. On the *Sueños* there are useful
theses by Goldenberg and Levisi (*23*, *27*), and an article by
Rovatti (*37*); Nolting-Hauff (*34*) has a good general study, noted
above. Probably the best studies of Quevedo's use of language
are those of Amédée Mas (*31*, ch.2) and Emilio Alarcos García
(*15*). My necessarily brief remarks are indebted to these scholars.

(i) Puns and Wordplay

At the lowest verbal level in the *Sueños* we find pun and
wordplay, with more examples than can be quoted (some have
been noted in the set-piece description of the doctors and
apothecaries considered above). At the level of the sound of
words is the joke about 'Sí, son' and 'sisón' (*sisón* itself has two
meanings) in *Juicio* (20, 136), and the joke on doctors, money,
and the title 'don' in *Muerte*: 'todos tienen don de matar, y
quieren más din, al despedirse que don al llamarlos' (196).

Quevedo exploits two meanings of the same word; the editor
of his poetry, González de Salas, thought him to be a poet
particularly rich in this kind of wordplay (*13*, vol.I, p.136). In
Infierno an *hidalgo* declares that he cannot be made to 'pagar
pecho' (122), so a devil makes him 'pagar espalda' (*pecho*, 'tax',
'chest'). Piemakers complain that 'nos condenamos por el
pecado de la carne, sin conocer mujer, tratando más en huesos'

(120). The joke is that they deny carnality by admitting that they put no meat in their pies. The cobblers in hell 'son los que vinieron consigo mismos, digo, en cueros. Y como otros se van al infierno por su pie, éstos se van por los ajenos y los suyos.' *En cueros* means 'naked' and *cuero*, 'leather'; there is also a play on 'por' in its different senses. These men go to hell for what they do to other people's feet. We also remember the play on *obras* ('literary productions' and 'deeds') made by the condemned bookseller in *Infierno* (116).

Some of these exploitations of senses of words approach wit, in the sense of connection of ideas. The kings in *Alguacil* are 'haciendo amazonas sus villas y ciudades a fuerza de grandes pechos, que en vez de criar, desustancian' (97). The bosoms of the Amazons are related to the effects of taxation; but *pechos* feed, in one sense, and in the other sense, taxes exhaust. There was also a tradition that the Amazons amputated one breast to be able to use bows; kings amputate towns by taxation. Quevedo uses mock-etymology at the level of wordplay, as in the joke in *Alguacil* about 'agua', 'alguacil', and 'merino', the old form for a constable, which they are alleged to have rejected for the Moorish word. The joke begins with words, but extends outwards towards racial enmity. In *Alguacil* Quevedo again attacks merchants, and uses a series of wordplays:

> habéis de saber que en España los misterios de los genoveses son dolorosos para los millones que vienen de las Indias, y que los cañones de sus plumas son de batería contra las bolsas; y no hay renta que, si la cogen en medio el tajo de sus plumas y el jarama de su tinta no la ahoguen. (98)

The Genoese were accused of exploiting the American gold and silver (the allusion is to the dolorous mysteries of the Virgin); *cañones* are 'cannons' and 'stems of quills'; *tajo* is a play on 'cut or slash' and the river Tagus; this leads on to the rivers (Jarama) of ink used by the Genoese.

The devil points sardonically to a play of words on *asiento* to make a joke which alludes to the accusation of homosexuality

made by contemporary Spaniards against Italians: 'han hecho
entre nosotros sospechosos este nombre de asiento, que como
significan traseros, no sabemos cuando hablan a lo negociante o
cuando a lo bujarrón' (99).

A final example, with serious undertones: when Quevedo sees
some buffoons in hell, he plays upon the senses of the word
gracia ('wit', 'divine grace'): 'Y repliqué yo cómo se
condenaban, y me respondieron que como se condenan otros
por no tener gracia, ellos se condenan por tenerla o quererla
tener' (118).

(ii) Metaphor

Quevedo's extraordinary use of metaphor has also been
studied by scholars, who have divided his metaphors into
various categories; one grouping is: humanizing, dehumanizing,
deflating, and exaggerating. Such categories are bound to
overlap, since metaphors can often be seen in different ways, but
they are valuable when they make us examine Quevedo's style
more closely. We have seen some of Quevedo's deflating metaphors in action — doctors are 'ponzoñas graduadas' (this, for
instance, might be seen as an exaggerating metaphor, their
killing propensities being over-emphasized). Quevedo meta-
morphoses tailors as the firewood of hell (96, 115), *dueñas* as the
frogs of hell (126, the metaphor is developed at length), notaries
as the *gatos* (*gato* meant 'thief' as well as 'cat'), and judges as its
tasty pheasants (99). The *cornudos* of *Muerte* are given a series
of deflating metaphors, which Quevedo explains: 'los maridos
... andarán hechos buhoneros de sus mujeres, alabando cada
uno a sus agujas' (210). They are the cheapjack sellers of their
wives, and praise their wares. Quevedo uses a popular phrase
and demotes the husbands to hawkers and their wives to articles.
Further:

> hay maridos linternas, muy compuestos, muy lucidos, muy
> bravos, que vistos de noche y a oscuras parecen estrellas, y
> llegados cerca son candelilla, cuerno y hierro. (210)

These husbands come home deliberately late, accompanied by

lanterns since the streets were dark — and to give plenty of warning. Lanterns were made of semi-transparent horn, and horns were the symbols of cuckoldry. The rapidity and compression of the explanations of the metaphor bring it close to wit. There is another example in the next sentence: 'Otros maridos hay jeringas, que apartadas traen, y llegando se apartan' (211). The husbands attract clients to their wives while they are away, and force clients away from their wives when they come home. With some metaphors Quevedo did not need to give an explanation: 'Todos los ajuares del infierno, las ropas y tocados de los condenados, estaban prendidos, en vez de clavos y alfileres, con alguaciles' (86).

He sometimes uses a string of metaphors, understood at once when we know the reputation of the target of the metaphor. The epitome of spongers, Don Diego de Noche, receives a withering series of apostrophes:

> ¡Oh, estómago aventurero! ¡Oh, gaznate de rapiña! ¡Oh, panza al trote! ¡Oh, susto de los banquetes! ¡Oh, mosca de los platos! ¡Oh, sacabocados de los señores! ¡Oh, tarasca de los convites y cáncer de las ollas! ¡Oh, sabañón de las cenas! ¡Oh, sarna de los almuerzos! ¡Oh, sarpullido del mediodía! (226)

These metaphors deflate and dehumanize him, reducing him to diseases, and at the same time exaggerate his function as the dread enemy of other people's food. It is hard to separate kinds of metaphor, but some at least are clearly based upon exaggeration. The attack upon talkers in *Muerte* is a clear example:

> Unos hablaban de hilván, otros a borbotones, otros a chorretadas, otros habladorísimos, hablan a cántaros. Gente que parece que lleva pujo de decir necedades, como si hubiera tomado alguna purga confeccionada de hojas de Calepino de ocho lenguas. Estos me dijeron que eran habladores diluvios, sin escampar de día ni de noche. (193)

Here Quevedo draws upon any frame of reference (sewing, water-flow, medicine, a famous dictionary, floods) to convey speed and quantity.

Exaggerated metaphor is usually comic in the *Sueños*, whereas deflating metaphor is more obviously satirical; we remember the widow's wake in a room so dark that they wept 'a tiento' (171), and the rich man in his carriage, so dignified and formal that he becomes more rigid and stiff than his own hat (this is also a dehumanizing metaphor):

> sumida la cara en un cuello abierto hacia arriba, que parecía vela en papel, y tan olvidado de sus coyunturas, que no sabía dónde volverse a hacer una cortesía ni levantar el brazo a quitarse el sombrero, el cual parecía miembro, según estaba fijo y firme. (177)

Probably one of the best examples of the exaggerated manner in the *Sueños* is the description of Dueña Quintañona, again a dehumanizing exercise:

> Con una cara hecha de un orejón, los ojos en dos cuévanos de vendimiar, la frente con tantas rayas y de tal color y hechura que parecía planta de pie; la nariz, en conversación con la barbilla, que casi juntándose hacían garra, y una cara de la impresión del grifo ... (223)

Her face is so wrinkled it looks like a piece of dried fruit, her eye-sockets are exaggerated into the dark cellars where wine is made; her forehead and the soles of her feet are linked by their wrinkles, her nose and her chin protrude so as to form a claw, her whole face is like some nightmarish griffin. Quevedo continues: 'la cabeza con temblor de sonajas, y la habla danzante; unas tocas muy largas sobre el monjil negro esmaltando de mortaja la tumba' (223). Her head is shaking like a timbrel (a kind of tambourine) and her speech is dancing or quivering to the music. She is wearing a nun's dress (a convention among *dueñas*) and the coif or wimple is white; her dress is the *tumba* which contains her dead body, and the coif reminds us of a shroud (*24*, pp.104, 136).

(iii) Wit

As we have seen, some of Quevedo's metaphor, when it is worked out at length, approaches wit, in the literary and seventeenth-century sense of *agudeza* and conceits. It is sometimes difficult to separate clever or outrageous metaphor from conceit, but the more explanation a metaphor demands, or the more connections of idea apparent in a passage, the nearer we are to wit. For instance, kings are mercury, according to the Marqués de Villena in *Muerte*, and he explains this deflating metaphor in detail (214-15). Pero Grullo offers a withering simile in *Muerte* also: women are like money, and he explains it, 'amigo de andar y que le manoseen y le obedezcan, enemigo de que le guarden' (218). One of the best passages of wit based on wordplay and allusion concerns the merchants in *Infierno*:

Estos ... son los que han ganado como buenos caballeros el infierno por sus pulgares, pues a puras pulgaradas se nos vienen acá. Mas, ¿quién duda que la oscuridad de sus tiendas les prometía estas tinieblas? Gente es ésta ... que quiso ser como Dios, pues pretendieron ser sin medida; mas El, que todo lo ve, los trajo de sus rasos a estos nublados que los atormenten con rayos. (122)

Irony, wordplay and wit all collaborate here. Using their thumbs to cheat while weighing or measuring, they have gained hell as well as profit (there may be some hint of the noble family name 'Pulgar' here but these are not 'buenos caballeros'); the darkness of their shops, which they exploited in order to cheat (an old accusation against shopkeepers, found in medieval satire) is connected with the darkness of hell; they lived abjuring measurements, and only God is beyond measure; *rasos* means 'silks' and, in *cielo raso*, clear sky; from their *rasos* they have been sent to this dark place, with thunderbolts dropping from the clouds. The basis of the wit is wordplay, but what is pointed at is the punishment of sin. In *Alguacil* Quevedo proposes a parallel between kinds of devil (fantastic) and kinds of constable (real); the testifying devil takes this up and agrees they have the same *oficio*. He makes a satirical distinction, however: 'los demonios lo fuimos por querer ser más que Dios, y los alguaciles son alguaciles por querer ser menos que todos' (91). The mocking parallel is essentially witty in its unlikely and explained appropriateness.

Quevedo parodies conceits when he meets a poet in hell, and we note that here at least he bases conceits upon words rather than ideas, although the underlying idea is that of the venality of women: 'Estas señoras hermosas, todas se han vuelto medio camareras de los hombres, pues los desnudan y no los visten' (140). Some conceits are evidently strained connections of ideas:

> el cruel resbalón que una lechigada de taberneros dio en las lágrimas que otros habían derramado en el camino, que por ser agua, se le fueron los pies y dieron en nuestra senda unos sobre otros. (109)

The basic idea is that innkeepers slide into hell because they water their wine, but the connections (water from tears of strugglers on the road of virtue, the water put into the wine, so that the tears of the repentant make others slide into hell) are awkward and even unfortunate.

One of the most deadly of the witty constructions occurs in the attack on piemakers:

> ¿Qué de estómagos pudieran ladrar, si resucitaran los perros que les hicistes comer? ¿Qué de dientes habéis hecho jinetes y qué de estómagos habéis traído a caballo, dándoles a comer rocines enteros? (121)

Teeth are horsemen and stomachs can bark, because piemen put horse and dog-meat into their pies; the reader is to connect the fraud with the teeth and the stomach.

Quevedo can also put up a witty metaphor, or a conceit, without warning or explanation; he says of a *cornudo*: 'como vuelve a su casa con un esquilón por tos tan sonora que se oye a seis calles' (183). The cuckold was symbolized by a horned animal, a ram or a goat (a deflating metaphor is the base here); the leading ram of a flock carries a bell around its neck; this man warns of his presence by a loud cough — his goat-bell.

One final example. Describing an old woman in *Alguacil*, Quevedo uses a conceit he also used in a satirical sonnet (*12*, p.572): 'y con tener ya amortajadas las sienes con la sábana blanca de sus canas y arada la frente ...' (101). The idea, in the middle of some traditional satire about old women, suddenly adds a darker note: her hair is white, like a shroud, already wrapped round her temples; her face is lined, ploughed like the earth; death has already seized a vain old woman.

4. Themes

a) Social

The wide range of themes and topics in the *Sueños*, and Quevedo's generally consistent attitudes to them, become apparent if we try to divide them into categories. Firstly, the social. As we have seen, Quevedo attacks, often with traditional insults, the tradesmen and the business men of his time: tailors, pastrycooks, innkeepers, coachmen, barbers, shoemakers. These are the trades of the capital and the royal court, with which a courtier like Quevedo would be familiar. He would despise these people for social and economic reasons; he might well have owed them money; they are motivated by profit, and cheat and over-charge. Furthermore, they might, by the purchase of titles, rise into the noble class, and thus be a danger to Quevedo's status and the status quo. In the *Hora de todos* (section 30) Quevedo shows some awareness of how money is made, but he belonged to a social class to which work and trade (but not unearned income) would be undignified. Quevedo's attack upon luxury trades (on jewellers in particular) is based not only on their possible dishonesty, but also on their pandering to and exploitation of vanity. They are selling things which are worthless when properly considered (122, 218, 219, 222); this attitude is close to the stoic and *desengañado* awareness that life is full of false appearances. This apparently trivial theme is thus connected with a serious moral attitude. At a higher financial level, Quevedo shared the xenophobic suspicion of his countrymen that Spain was being bled by international financiers, to whom monopolies and official contracts were granted in return for loans to the crown. A satirist is not compelled to analyse his country's problems more closely.

Quevedo also attacks the professions, again in the medieval and classical traditions of satire. In his own lawsuits he had had experience of the dilatoriness, unreliability, and venality of lawyers, and the corruption of judges, notaries, and the police. (Cervantes attacks these aspects of the law in *Rinconete y Cortadillo* and in *El coloquio de los perros*.) There may be some social resentment here also. *Hidalgos* were exempt from some taxes but they were not above the law (although it was well known that the rich could influence the application of the law). Quevedo's class tended to be involved in lawsuits about property and status; they were aware that the law was a means of social and financial advancement for socially inferior but intelligent and unscrupulous men. Quevedo returns to the subject in the *Hora de todos*, section 19, for a final re-working.

Quevedo's satire against doctors, apothecaries, surgeons and dentists is again part of traditional satire and also the result of personal experience. He repeats the traditional insult that doctors and dentists live by ruining the health of others, and he notes the misuse of language, as well as of medical ingredients, by apothecaries and *ensalmadores*.

A number of other attacks at this social level are motivated by personal dislikes and the paying-off of individual scores. Sensitive to the use of language, Quevedo classifies 'habladores' as killers. This is both a personal phobia and part of the satirical tradition; on different levels of seriousness St Paul and Horace both attack idle talkers. He had considerable experience of the royal court and of ambitious and backbiting courtiers. The attack on *chismosos*, *mentirosos*, and *entremetidos* is a kind of revenge for the conditions and vicissitudes of his own career. He returns to the theme in the *Discurso de todos los diablos*, where there is a memorable picture of Lucifer as a statesman, with papers in his hatband, and in the *Hora de todos* (sections 15 and 21). He attacks one or two personal enemies in the *Sueños* — the fencing-master in *Juicio*, the bookseller in *Infierno*, and the *licenciado* Calabrés, although he is presented somewhat ambiguously. He attacks the widespread appropriation of the title 'don' (196) — a satirical commonplace of the time, and also, probably, a matter of personal resentment. He mocks the parasitical pseudo-gentleman of the time in the figure of Don Diego de Noche (226) and in the comic *caballero* in *Juicio* (84).

Gentlemen who were unwilling or unable to work and who were unwilling to forgo their claims to status were a social problem of the time; the type is observed in *Lazarillo de Tormes*. Quevedo, as a gentleman without wealth or title, may have felt himself a little too near these people for comfort, but in the *Sueños* he sees only the funny and cruel side of the problem. In the *Hora de todos* he sardonically recommends such people to crime, which will lead either to wealth or to execution; in the *Epístola satírica y censoria* (lines 130-33) he looks back more constructively to a time when work was honourable. On a more moral level he attacks the major fetishes of the *hidalgo* (*honra, sangre, valentía*) in *Infierno*.

Quevedo's attacks upon women in poetry and prose have earned him the reputation of a misogynist, although it should be borne in mind that he was also one of the greatest love poets of the language, and that *Muerte* and the *Heráclito cristiano* are dedicated respectfully to ladies. Satire of women is very ancient, and Quevedo uses ideas from Juvenal, Persius, and Martial on the subject. We cannot speculate on any personal motives. He attacks old women who pretend to be young, heavily made-up women (the most calculated example is in *Dentro*), the venality of women, and the hypocrisy of *dueñas*. He is sceptical about the grief of widows, and also of widowers. He is sarcastic about complaisant cuckolds; this implies an attack on their wives, who are seen as partners in a commercial partnership. Quevedo's attacks upon cosmetics, lying marriage-brokers, and false marriages can be seen as part of the Stoic denunciation of false appearances, as well as part of the satirical tradition.

In the *Sueños* and in the *Discurso de todos los diablos* we also find attacks on specific figures of the immediate and distant past. He attacks alchemists, geomancers, and astrologers, whose alleged science was by now close to total discredit, although they were an important part of the intellectual life of the preceding two centuries. Frances A. Yates (*43*) refers to a number of magicians mentioned by Quevedo. He seems to know their work quite well, as Mas and Martinengo have observed (*30, 31*), and they were still attracting official interest in the seventeenth century (*14*, p.462). Quevedo is taking part here in one of the useful functions of satire — the clearing-away of absurd science and obfuscation. The pseudo-scientists are found in *Infierno* near the long list of heretics (151-53) that Quevedo took, with some comments of his own, from an old book on them. The heretics provided him with some safe fun at the expense of people appropriately consigned to hell. Mohammed, Luther, and Judas Iscariot receive more thoughtful treatment. Mohammed condemns himself and his followers with vigour; Quevedo argues with Luther about images, faith, and works (the satirist occasionally needs to demonstrate that he is in fact a person of sound opinion, despite his posture of disrespect). Raimundo Lida (*29*) and Jean Vilar (*42*) have studied the profound attraction the figure of Judas had for Quevedo. The minor heretics are safe satirical subjects flippantly dealt with (satire was meant to amuse); on the other hand, outdated science, Lutheranism, and Islam were serious subjects for a Spaniard of the time.

Some contemporary and traditional subjects of satire are not found in the *Sueños*, and their absence reveals something about Quevedo as a satirist. There is no real satire on the church, in contrast to *Lazarillo* or the *Diálogo de Mercurio y Carón*, for instance. One direct attack in *Juicio* was cut by the censors (*10*, p.183), but otherwise there is very little to compare even with the sly remarks to be found occasionally in Cervantes. The attack on the hypocritical *licenciado* Calabrés is evidently personal rather than general, and the original was apparently a fair target. The attack on hypocritical holy men and their ambiguous devotees is unexceptionable — they would have been legitimate targets of a preacher; even so, the attack was reduced in force for the *Juguetes* (see *7*, vol.I, p.101). Quevedo was a devout Christian, as the volume and quality of his devotional writing testifies; he expresses his respect for the Jesuits who had educated him; and he was writing, at the time of the earlier *Sueños*, some moving religious poetry. The *Juguetes* revision is in part the result of criticisms of the *Sueños* by certain clerical enemies (even though most of these criticisms are wrong-headed and absurd); no doubt he also authorized a half-hearted revision in order to avoid trouble with the Inquisition. His adherence to

Roman Catholic beliefs however need not be doubted; he would thus not see the Church as a target for satire.

Nor is he very critical in the area of politics. As we have seen, the devil in *Alguacil* reports that there are kings in hell surrounded by their entourages (97-98); their sins are extreme because of their position, but Quevedo is cautious enough to except Spanish kings from the damned; Maldonado notes some possible ironies in the passage, which was also revised for the *Juguetes* edition. We have also seen that the Marqués de Villena makes a number of comments about the politics of around 1621, but these remarks are partly flattery of the king, and partly one view of a political dilemma of the time; the passage was again modified for the *Juguetes* version (*7*, vol.I, p.235). Quevedo's political remarks in the *Sueños* are mild compared with some of the satirical verse of the time. There has been some recent discussion and scepticism about Quevedo as a political critic. He certainly seems to be satirizing aspects of the reign of Felipe III in the first part of his *Política de Dios*, but it was not published until ten years after it was written, as Jean Vilar points out (*42*). The second part, which criticises aspects of the reign of Felipe IV, was published after Quevedo's death. Some parts of the *Hora de todos*, written in the 1630s, are critical of the policies of Olivares (see *14*, introduction), but this also was published posthumously. Quevedo's political views, and his need to protect his career, probably precluded any real political satire in the *Sueños*.

b) Language and literature

Satirists are often critical of the spoken language and the literature of their time, and these are major interests of Quevedo in the *Sueños*. On the literary level, he mocks prologues and fawning preliminary notes to the unknown reader. He mocks bad poets, and parodies bad poetry (he was himself a poet of established reputation by the time of the earlier *Sueños*). He mocks the silly clichés of the theatre of his time. His various hells are inhabited by writers of books, and this includes the astrologers, necromancers, and heretics. He is also contemptuous of books of jurisprudence in his satire against lawyers (212), and he regards some historians as mere flatterers in print (158), an idea he expands in *Discurso*. In *Infierno* he consigns a bookseller to hell, as a tradesman, a purveyor of immorality, and a diffuser of popular culture. He also expresses, as we have seen, a sense of the purpose of writing in *Muerte* and at the end of *Dentro*.

Quevedo also reveals his interest in the spoken language throughout the *Sueños* (35). He notes the false and flattering names given to things (125, 166, another satirical topos) and he comments upon the tendency of quack doctors to use solecisms of language (144). More seriously, he points to the lethal foolishness of silly phrases like 'pensé que' and 'es cosa de risa' (201). This irritated sensitivity to foolish phrases comes to a climax in *Muerte*, where a number of such phrases point angrily to their significance. He returns obsessively to this theme in *Discurso de todos los diablos* and in the *Hora de todos*, and wrote a short story, *El cuento de cuentos*, almost entirely in catch-phrases in order to clean up his own language, in the prologue of which he says:

> Yo, por no andar rascando mi lenguaje todo el día, he querido espulgar de una vez en esta jornada, donde yo solo no tengo qué hacer. Y en este cuento he sacado a la vergüenza todo el asco de nuestra conversación. (*10*, p.773)

This is not only a personal obsession. In the view of the time, speech was one of the things which separated men from animals. Fray Luis de León in *De los nombres de Cristo* (1583) writes at length on the importance of language; the dogs in *El coloquio de los perros* refer to 'el divino don de la palabra'. Satirists often see corrupt language as a sign of corruption in society; the Newspeak of George Orwell's *1984* is a modern example. The importance given to the *chistes* in the last of the *Sueños* is not therefore a descent in satirical or moral seriousness; as an artist of language Quevedo could never underestimate its power or its misuse.

c) Moral and religious

Finally, one of the major features of the *Sueños* is, clearly, the quantity and the quality of the moral writing. Ilse Nolting-Hauff (*34*, p.122) illuminatingly observes that the *Sueños* are often close to contemporary devotional writing, especially meditations on death, the Last Judgement, and hell (the *postrimerías*, or Last Things).[15] This profoundly affects the style of some passages in the *Sueños*. In the first, where Quevedo is to some extent trying out a mode of writing, there is little direct sermonizing; the satirical device is the message — the sins of men will be judged before God, however petty they may seem, and however wittily they are presented. In *Alguacil* the devil tells the morally significant story of Truth and Justice, and makes some effective remarks on the absence of the poor from hell. In *Infierno* there are discourses about military conduct and rewards, hypocrisy, honour, bravery, noble blood, and true and false prayer. One of the damned, in a passage characteristic of a meditation on the pains of hell, is tormented by the memory of the good he could have done.

In *Dentro* the moral element is vitally important. Quevedo's own *desengaño* preaches to him about the world of false appearances and about the relation of sin to hypocrisy; he reminds us of the passage of time and of the inexorable approach of death; he mocks even learning when it is separated from prudence. In *Muerte* Quevedo and Death talk about the true nature of death, and the reader is shown the horror of the world, the flesh, the devil, and money. The apparently comic *chistes* reveal that they are not comic and are not meaningless when properly considered. The element of moral teaching is not allowed to swamp the *Sueños*, but Quevedo's interest in the truth of matters, from the alleged contents of meat pies, through apparent honour, to the true nature of prayer, reminds us that the correct, disabused, view of things, and awareness of the

---

[15] She offers a number of interesting parallels between moral passages of the *Sueños* and passages from contemporary and earlier devotional writers and preachers, notably Diego de Estella, Fray Luis de Granada, the Beato Juan de Avila, and Fray Alonso de Cabrera (*34*, pp.160-83).

deceits of the world, are major preoccupations of the Christian
and Stoic writers of the time.[16]

---

[16] Besides *La cuna y la sepultura*, mentioned earlier, he also wrote works with
titles like *Virtud militante contra las cuatro pestes del mundo: Invidia,
Ingratitud, Soberbia, Avaricia* (1634-36) and *La providencia de Dios* (1641-42).

5. Conclusion

Looking at the *Sueños* as a whole, we should bear in mind the element of traditional satire, inherited from the Classics, medieval writing, and contemporaries. The *Sueños* would have seemed funnier in their time than they do now, and the fun would be instantly rather than laboriously appreciated. Even at our distance in time we can see the comic force of the frequent reversal of expectations — the devils who preach and are snobbish about the police, the poets punished by hearing the work of other poets, and who are trapped by the demands of rhyme; the parody of ingratiating prologues and sycophantic addresses to the reader; the ungrieved attitudes of mourners.

Probably the most obvious, and difficult, feature of the *Sueños* is the brilliant verbal style, a major element of Quevedo's reputation even today. It is necessary to read each sentence with care, to pick up the wordplay, the allusions, the ironies, the sudden deadly adjective where it is not expected, the complex wit. It often seems that Quevedo's interest in the use and misuse of language is more important to him than his interest in moral discourse.

Some modern critics (*22, 33, 42*) have seen Quevedo's consciousness of his social status as an important element of his writing, and in particular of his satire. We have seen that he is apparently resentful of social climbers, and suspicious of foreigners, heretics, lawyers, tradesmen, bankers, *nouveaux riches*, and social change in general. At the same time he is cautious in his criticisms of the church and the accepted social order. In modern terms he can be accused of being an elitist and a snob. These aspects of the *Sueños* may certainly be a reflection of his position in society. We should also bear in mind, probably, that the *Sueños* are mainly the work of a young man; we have an impression of a talented and flippant young man about the royal court, with a reputation as a poet and a wit, who is trying to attract attention as a handy pen, a right-thinking satirist, not without his serious side, and not really a ferocious critic of the status quo. *Muerte* has a more sombre tone as if Quevedo is turning towards a more profound examination of the failings of men and of the meaning of language. The deeper satire of Quevedo comes later in his career.

Although Quevedo's satire in the *Sueños* is traditional and conventional, and although it avoids some areas of interest to earlier and later satirists, it is obviously an important element of the work. There is a respectable tradition of conservative satire, which expresses the general idea that things are not as healthy as they were, that they are in fact going to the dogs, and in this sense and within the limits he chose, Quevedo is a satirist, probably the greatest in Spanish until the nineteenth century. Some aspects of the satire apply to all societies: incompetent doctors and corrupt tradesmen, lawyers, and policemen did and do exist; language could and can be used to evade issues; false appearances are not unheard of today. Certain aspects of the society of Quevedo's time are being judged, damned, and consigned to hell in the *Sueños*; failings of men of that time, not eradicated in our time, are attacked here by a ruthless and brilliant pen. The passages of moral writing in the last three *Sueños* add a universal element, making the *Sueños* as a whole much more than a series of clever verbal exercises on traditional topics of satire.

Appendix: Editions of the Sueños

The editorial history of the *Sueños* is complex; the best account of the manuscripts, the printed editions, and their revisions is to be found in Amédée Mas (*8*), to which the following summary is indebted.

Quevedo wrote the five *Sueños* between 1605 and 1622. As was the custom of the time, copies of the manuscripts were passed around among friends, and copies were made, of varying accuracy. Some important manuscripts have survived (*8*, pp.9-12) although none is an autograph. Astrana Marín (*10*) publishes *censuras* of two early *Sueños* of 1610, apparently for a projected edition, but no printed edition of the *Sueños* is known before 1627.

In 1627 the five *Sueños* were published in Barcelona, with the title *Sueños y discursos de verdades descubridoras de abusos, vicios y engaños, en todos los oficios y estados del mundo.* This important first edition was apparently not supervised or authorized by Quevedo. The long general prologue (*6*, pp.65-70) is probably by the bookseller, Juan Sapera, and the five pieces are entitled *El sueño del juicio final* (1605?); *El alguacil endemoniado* (1605-08?) *El sueño del infierno* (1608); *El mundo por de dentro* (1612); and *El sueño de la muerte* (1622). Three of the dates are given by the texts; it is usually assumed that the *Sueños* were written in this order. This edition also included a comic and satirical work by Quevedo, *Cartas del caballero de la tenaza*, and a comic poem. The general prologue by Sapera is not without interest; it makes a number of conventional statements about satire:

> a todos habla, y a todos dice la verdad clara y lisa, y lo que siente, sin rastro de lisonja; y si acaso escuece y pica, considere que no es sino sólo porque cuanto se dice es verdad y desengaño. (67)

Sapera declares that he was urged to publish his version for excellent reasons:

> asegurándome grande gusto y lo que más es, grande provecho espiritual para todos, pues en ellos hallarán desengaños y avisos de lo que pasa en este mundo y ha de pasar en el otro. (69)

Other editions followed in the same year, 1627, notably those published in Zaragoza and Valencia. Also in Zaragoza and in the same year (perhaps, as Maldonado says (*6*, p.39) as the result of rivalry between booksellers to publish a best-seller), a version of the *Sueños* was published with the title of *Desvelos soñolientos y verdades soñadas*. This contains only three of the *Sueños* (*Muerte*, *Juicio*, and *Infierno*, in that order), and gives, in its omissions and additions, a somewhat different version of the text of the three pieces (*8*, p.18). A friend of Quevedo, Lorenzo van der Hammen, wrote a letter published with this edition in which he refers to the bad state of the extant manuscripts and claims to have corrected them ('por los originales que en mi librería tengo, y aun yo mismo he escrito gran parte, como lo dirá la letra', 59). This edition is used to clarify some passages of the text of *Muerte* in the Maldonado edition (*6*). Juan Sapera edited a version of the *Sueños* in 1628 in which he collates the first *Sueños* and the *Desvelos* (*8*, p.19).

Editions of both these versions of the *Sueños* were published in the following two years. Some literary enemies of Quevedo, who objected to various irreverent passages, endeavoured to have the book placed on the Index of the Inquisition. Quevedo apparently tried to anticipate them by denouncing these early editions not authorized by him. In 1629 he authorized, and assisted in some parts of the publication of, an official and acceptable version of the *Sueños*, helped by a friend, Alonso Messia de Leiva. This appeared in Madrid in 1631, with the title *Juguetes de la niñez y travessuras del ingenio*. It includes all five *Sueños* although the titles of four are changed: *Juicio* becomes *El sueño de las calaveras*; *Alguacil* becomes *El alguacil alguacilado*; *Infierno* becomes *Las zahurdas de Plutón*; *Muerte*

becomes *La visita de los chistes.* (*Dentro* keeps the same title.)
The *Juguetes* also include *El entremetido, la dueña y el soplón*,
later called *El discurso de todos los diablos*. In the prologue,
Messia de Leiva claims to have original manuscripts of the
Sueños, and so he is able to improve on the first edition. He
points out that Quevedo was not responsible for the first edition,
and had himself asked the Inquisition to ban the earlier editions.
He notes the nature of the corrections: 'en todas se ha excusado
la mezcla de lugares de la Sagrada Escritura y alguna licencia
que no era apacible. Que, aunque hoy se lee uno y otro en
Dante, Don Francisco me ha permitido esta lima' (*7*, vol.I,
p.18). The general intention was evidently to remove the
irreverences of the early edition, some of which may have crept
into the manuscripts as they were copied and recopied. The
corrections are carried out rather woodenly at times, notably in
Juicio, which contains a number of references to divine figures,
hastily changed to pagan gods, so that, for instance, Judas is
said to have betrayed Jupiter. There are, however, some
important cuts, additions, and replacements. For instance, the
Mundo por de dentro ends abruptly in early versions; in the
Juguetes, a final reprise passage is added, written by Quevedo
himself. The passage about hypocrites with its references to the
Scriptures is modified. This improves the coherence of the
writing at times, as well as making the work acceptable to
religious readers. Despite the evident absurdity or pointlessness
of many of the minor corrections, the *Juguetes* edition
represents an important stage in the history of the *Sueños*. It is
the only version authorized by Quevedo, and it authenticates
most of the text of the edition of 1627; indeed the corrections are
such that the reader must at times turn to the earlier versions for
the proper sense.

In the eighteenth century an attempt was made to conflate the
two main editions, but the next important edition of the *Sueños*
came in 1852, with the version in the complete works of
Quevedo published by Aureliano Fernández Guerra (*9*). This
scholar used the *Juguetes* (in a late edition) for his basis, but he
was aware of the original *Sueños*, in an edition published in
Pamplona; he also drew to some extent on manuscript sources

(*8*, p.34). The Clásicos Castellanos edition of the *Sueños* (*7*) copies Fernández Guerra faithfully, and although it is not a true scholarly edition by modern standards it gives the student some idea of the *Juguetes* version in the main text, and of the 1627 *Sueños* in the footnotes.

In 1932 Luis Astrana Marín published the prose works of Quevedo (*10* is a reprint, of 1945) with an edition of the *Sueños* based upon manuscript sources and Fernández Guerra. In 1955 Amédée Mas published a genuinely scholarly edition of one *Sueño*, *Las zahurdas de Plutón* (formerly *Infierno*) with full and meticulous references to manuscripts and the early printed sources, and the important bibliographical study which I have drawn upon here. The best modern edition of the *Sueños* available to students is that of Felipe C.R. Maldonado (*6*); this is based upon Barcelona, 1627, and draws upon the *Juguetes* and the *Desvelos*. James O. Crosby has for some years been working on an edition of the *Sueños*; its publication will be an important stage in our knowledge of the text.

Bibliographical Note

A. GENERAL BIBLIOGRAPHY OF CRITICAL WORKS

J.O. Crosby, *Guía bibliográfica para el estudio crítico de Quevedo*, Research Bibliographies and Checklists, 13 (London: Grant and Cutler, 1976).

B. BACKGROUND WORKS

1. Bleznick, D.W., *Quevedo*, Twayne's World Authors Series, 153 (New York: Twayne, 1972).
2. Elliott, J.H., *Imperial Spain, 1469-1716* (London: Arnold, 1963).
3. Lynch, John, *Spain under the Habsburgs*, 2 vols, second edition (Oxford: Blackwell, 1981).
4. Paulson, Ronald (editor), *Satire: Modern Essays in Criticism* (Englewood Cliffs, N.J.: Prentice Hall, 1971).
5. Scholberg, K.R., *Sátira e invectiva en la España medieval* (Madrid: Gredos, 1971).

C. TEXTS OF QUEVEDO'S WORKS

6. *Sueños y discursos de verdades descubridoras de abusos, vicios y engaños en todos los oficios y estados del mundo*, edited by Francisco L.R. Maldonado (Madrid: Castalia, 1972). Interesting introduction and useful bibliography. See Appendix, p.83.
7. *Los sueños*, edited by Julio Cejador y Frauca, 2 vols, Clásicos Castellanos, 31 and 34 (Madrid: La Lectura, 1916-17; repr. Madrid: Espasa-Calpe, 1942-43). Also reprinted at later dates; quotations in this Guide are from the 1942-43 reprint.
8. *Las zahurdas de Plutón* (*El sueño del infierno*), edited by Amédée Mas (Poitiers: Texier, 1955).
9. *Obras en prosa*, I, edited by Aurelio Fernández Guerra, Biblioteca de Autores Españoles, 23 (Madrid: Rivadeneyra, 1852).
10. *Obras completas en prosa*, edited by Luis Astrana Marín (Madrid: Espasa-Calpe, 1945).
11. *Obras completas, obras en verso*, edited by Luis Astrana Marín (Madrid: Espasa-Calpe, 1943).
12. *Obras completas, I, Poesía original*, edited by José Manuel Blecua (Barcelona: Planeta, 1968).
13. *Obra poética*, edited by José Manuel Blecua, 4 vols (Madrid: Castalia, 1969-81).

14. L'Heure de tous (La hora de todos), edited by Jean Bourg, Pierre Dupont, and Pierre Genest (Paris, Aubier, 1980).

D. CRITICISM

15. Alarcos García, Emilio, 'Quevedo y la parodia idiomática', *Archivum*, 5 (1955), 3-38. Important study of Quevedo's style; a short account of this article appears in Mas (*31*).

16. Asensio, Eugenio, *Itinerario del entremés, desde Lope de Rueda a Quiñones de Benavente* (Madrid: Gredos, 1965). Contains some useful incidental comments on the *Sueños*.

17. Canal Feijoo, C.A., 'El tema del sueño y la imagen del laberinto en Quevedo', in Cvitanovic, see no.*19* below (pp.130-41). Account of the dream and labyrinthine elements in the *Sueños*.

18. Corbatta, Jorgelina, 'La fealdad de la figura humana en los *Sueños* de Quevedo', in *19*, pp.155-65. Lucid essay on how Quevedo describes people in the *Sueños*.

19. Cvitanovic, Dinko, *El sueño y su representación en el Barroco español* (Bahía Blanca: Cuadernos del Sur, 1969). Includes articles by Canal Feijoo, Corbatta, and Frentzel Beyme noted here. Cvitanovic's own article, 'Hipótesis sobre la signficación del sueño en Quevedo, Calderón y Shakespeare', pp.9-89, contains useful comments on each *sueño*, as well as some comparative study.

20. Ettinghausen, Henry, *Francisco de Quevedo and the Neostoic Movement* (London: Oxford University Press, 1972). Thorough account of Quevedo's Stoicism; final chapter refers illuminatingly to the *Sueños*.

21. Frentzel Beyme, Susana, 'Ejemplaridad de la figura humana en los *Sueños* de Quevedo', in *19*, pp.142-54.

22. Geisler, Eberhard, *Geld bei Quevedo. Zur Identitätskrise der Feudalgesellschaft im fruhen 17. Jahrhundert* (Frankfurt am Main: Lang, 1981). Study of Quevedo's attitude to money and wealth, with interesting comments on his social attitudes.

23. Goldenberg, Barbara B., 'Quevedo's *Sueños*: a stylistic analysis' (unpublished dissertation, Columbia University, 1951); summary in *Dissertation Abstracts*, 12 (1952), 3341.

24. Iffland, James, *Quevedo and the Grotesque*, I (London: Tamesis, 1978). Excellent study of Quevedo's style in prose and poetry; discusses passages from the *Sueños*.

25. Iventosch, Herman, 'Quevedo and the Defence of the Slandered', *Hispanic Review*, 30 (1962), 94-115 and 173-93. Two articles which show how Quevedo uses *Muerte* and the *Entremés de los refranes* to allow maligned figures, including *chistes*, to defend themselves.

26. Levisi, Margarita, 'Hieronymus Bosch y los *Sueños* de Quevedo', *Filología*, 9 (1963), 163-200. Interesting account of elements in common between Bosch and Quevedo; cautious about any direct connection.

27. ——, 'Los *Sueños* de Quevedo. El estilo, el humor, el arte' (unpublished dissertation, Ohio State University, 1965); summary in *Dissertation Abstracts*, 25 (1964-65), 1198. Good account of verbal style and humour in the *Sueños*.

28. Lida, Raimundo, 'Dos *Sueños* de Quevedo y un prólogo', in *Actas del Segundo Congreso Internacional de Hispanistas* (Nijmegen: Instituto Español de la Universidad, for AIH, 1967), pp.93-107. About *Alguacil*, the figure of Judas Iscariot in the *Sueños*, some remarks on the *Hora de todos*.

29. ——, '*Sueños y discursos*: el predicador y sus máscaras', in *Homenaje a Julio Caro Baroja*, ed. A. Carreira (Madrid: Centro de Investigaciones Sociológicas, 1978), pp.669-84. Good survey of the *Sueños*, especially on Quevedo's moral aims; includes remarks on *Discurso*.

30. Martinengo, Alessandro, *Quevedo e il simbolo alchimistico: tre studi* (Padua: Liviana, 1967). On Quevedo's knowledge of alchemy; second essay is a useful study of his style; third essay is on his poetic theory.

31. Mas, Amédée, *La Caricature de la femme, du mariage et de l'amour dans l'œuvre de Quevedo* (Paris: Ediciones Hispano-Americanas, 1957). Important account of these themes, and interesting stylistic study.

32. Morreale, Margherita, 'Luciano y Quevedo: la humanidad condenada', *Revista de Literatura*, 8 (1955), 213-27. Quevedo's echoes of satirical material of Lucian and his sixteenth-century imitators.

33. Müller, F.W., 'Allegorie und Realismus in den *Sueños* von Quevedo', *Archiv für das Studium der neueren Sprachen und Literaturen*, 202 (1966), 321-46; translated and included in *39*, pp.218-41. Very interesting on Quevedo's social status and attitudes.

34. Nolting-Hauff, Ilse, *Visión, sátira y agudeza en los 'Sueños' de Quevedo* (Madrid: Gredos, 1974), translation of *Vision, Satire und Pointe in Quevedos 'Sueños'* (Munich: Fink Verlag, 1968). A most important and thorough study of the *Sueños*; deals comprehensively with them as 'pseudo-narrations', and with satirical content and techniques.

35. Price, R.M., 'Quevedo's Satire on the Use of Words in the *Sueños*', *Modern Langauge Notes*, 78 (1964), 169-80. An account of Quevedo's interest in language, spoken and written, in the *Sueños*.

36. Pring-Mill, R.D.F., 'Some Techniques of Representation in the *Sueños* and the *Criticón*', *Bulletin of Hispanic Studies*, 45 (1968), 270-84. Profound study of techniques of representation in seventeenth-century prose, with reference to *Dentro*, the *Hora de todos*, *Guzmán de Alfarache* and the *Criticón*.

37. Rovatti, Loretta, 'Struttura e stile nei *Sueños* di Quevedo', *Studi Mediolatini e Volgari*, 15-16 (1968), 121-67. A good overall study of the *Sueños*.

38. Serrano, Carlos, 'Signe et allegorie: le *Mundo por de dentro* de Quevedo', *Les Langues Neo-Latines*, 70 (1976), 5-30. Scholarly analysis of the use of language in *Dentro*.

39. Sobejano, Gonzalo (editor), *Francisco de Quevedo* (Madrid: Taurus, 1978). A very useful collection of studies on Quevedo's prose and poetry; it includes the articles by Müller (*33*) and Vilar (*42*).

40. Spearing, A.C., *Medieval Dream-Poetry* (Cambridge: Cambridge University Press, 1976). Important study of medieval literary dream convention in English and French poems; many features are clearly applicable to the *Sueños*.

41. Ugalde, Victoriano, 'El narrador y los *Sueños* de Quevedo', *Revista Canadiense de Estudios Hispánicos*, 4 (1979-80), 183-95. Study of relation between author and narrator in the *Sueños*.

42. Vilar, Jean, 'Judas selon Quevedo: dispensero, ministro, arbitrista', in *Mélanges offerts a Charles V. Aubrun* (Paris: Editions Hispaniques, 1975), II, pp.385-97. Included in *39*, pp.106-11. Interesting account of Quevedo's cautious political attitudes and his treatments of Judas Iscariot.

43. Yates, Frances A., *Giordano Bruno and the Hermetic Tradition* (London: Routledge and Kegan Paul, 1964). Important study; useful for the background of the magicians and geomancers in *Infierno*.

CRITICAL GUIDES TO SPANISH TEXTS

Edited by
J.E. Varey and A.D. Deyermond